# Sex, Drugs &
# Rock 'n Roll

## Healing Today's Troubled Youth

## Paul King, M.D.
### with Jackie Flaum

ISBN: 0-922352-00-3

Library of Congress Catalog Card Number: 88-63440

Printed in the United States of America

Cover illustration:
Rosemary Dontje-Oehlerich

## ACKNOWLEDGEMENTS

Every seemingly new approach to problems actually has a history of antecedents. First, my gratitude to Dr. James Masterson, my professor in psychiatry at Cornell; my Twelve Step higher power, Vicki V.; tough-love parents like Nancy and Rick D.; and the adolescents who taught me about the power of drugs and rock-'n-roll. I am also grateful to Charter Medical Corporation — in particular to President William A. Fickling Jr., Vice President Charles Smith, Conference Coordinator Pat Fields, and to Administrator Sherry Thornton and the rest of the staff at Charter Lakeside Hospital. My publisher, Ed Hearn, had the faith to see the project through and the patience to keep me on track. Finally, to my wife, Nadine, and our children, Marc and Scott.

# Sex, Drugs & Rock 'n Roll

## CONTENTS

# INTRODUCTION

"At a time when professional groups have compartmentalized the human person into a jumbled assembly of parts, a time when different sets of technical jargon and terminology replace each other monthly, Dr. Paul King's book, "SEX, DRUGS & ROCK 'N ROLL...Healing Today's Troubled Youth" descends on us like a well of water to those dying of thirst.

If any addiction deprives its victims of the ability to love and be loved — the purpose of human existence — because it robs them of the freedom to be loved, then any therapy worthy of the name must of its nature set other people free to be able to restore the lost relationships with God, self, and others. The twelve principles of AA are geared to this. In Dr. Bob's own six-word summary of the steps, he spells it out with simplicity and clarity: Trust God (1, 2, 3); Clean House (4 through 11); Help Others (Step 12).

Living in a world of "do your own thing," a world where values shift and change on the sea of permissiveness, our young yearn and hunger for absolute standards to live by, anchors of security that will never change. They yearn for the authority and loving discipline their parents OWE them.

This book helps parents understand their job and gives them hints, help and hope for their awesome task of molding the character of their children. It stands as a monument of simplicity in a field loaded with repetition of side-issues cloaked in hard-to-understand gobbledegook. Dr. King is unafraid of criticism that might arise from those who feel this book is "too simple."

It is written in ordinary language, understandable by ordinary people like you and me. It is written, however, by an extraordinary man who has that rare ability to grasp the obvious and the rarer ability to pass it on.

This book is a gem; I suggest you read it."

**Father Joseph Martin**

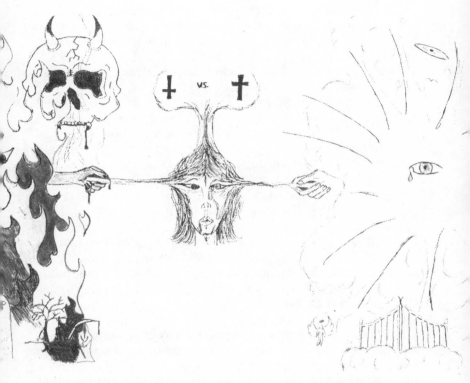

*This illustration represents the view of treatment offered by a 16-year-old Satan worshipper. Illustrations at beginnings of chapters were drawn by young people during treatment at Charter Lakewide Hospital, Memphis, Tennessee, under the care of the author, Paul King, M.D.*

# CHAPTER ONE

# The Alarm: Disconnected Young People

A CAR SCREECHES INTO THE DRIVEWAY, ITS STEREO BLARING heavy metal music into a quiet neighborhood. Someone gets out of the car, and a glass bottle smashes in the street to the sound of raucous laughter. The front door slams and up the carpeted stairs staggers a 15-year-old boy past curfew again. This night, like several others before, his mother lies in bed pretending to be asleep. She doesn't want another loud confrontation on the steps that might wake a younger sister or brother. She's afraid. So she lies in bed berating herself, blaming her ex-husband and hating what her family has become.

In another part of town, a doctor and his wife are relaxing after a gourmet dinner with friends. The telephone rings, and a nurse asks them to come to the emergency room. Their 17-year-old daughter got drunk and wrecked her car. The doctor and his wife are paralyzed with shock. Their beautiful, sweet daughter with straight As and a cheerleader uniform in the closet is a drunk driver? How is that possible?

Whether it is the White House Conference for a Drug Free America, a program with the U.S. surgeon general at the National Press Club, a meeting of the National Federation of Parents for Drug Free Youth, a workshop of the American Society for Adolescent Psychiatry, or a local PTA meeting, the questions I'm asked about adolescent drug and alcohol abuse are full of pain and desperation. Parents, elected officials, and colleagues are looking for answers to why youngsters resort to

1

drugs or alcohol, what can be done to stop teenage substance abuse, how the government can play a more effective role, and how to recognize a youngster who has a problem with chemicals.

The parents who come to me with these questions are frightened for their own youngsters, the public officials are trying to formulate policy to handle a national crisis, and my colleagues in the alcohol and drug counseling field are struggling to understand an age group for which they are unprepared. Those with child mental health training refuse to see chemical abuse as a primary disturbance rather than a combination of problems.

These adults do well to be concerned. Nationally, the situation is alarming. Almost two-and-a-half million American youngsters now can be classified as "disconnected youth," according to the *Washington Post* in 1985. They have no strong ties to their families, their schools, their jobs – and often, to reality.

Figures from the Education Commission of the States show that, since 1960, drug and alcohol problems among adolescents have increased 60 times; a million teens become pregnant every year; homicides among white youth are up 23 percent; among blacks they are up 16 percent. The teenage suicide rate is up 150 percent – a teenager commits suicide every 90 minutes in this country (*Washington Post,* 1985). Nearly 70 percent of these suicides are among persons below age 30 with histories of drug or alcohol abuse (Fowler, 1986). Well over 60 percent of the pregnancies, homicides, and juvenile crime can be traced to the use of drugs or alcohol, police and social service workers believe. In Houston, for example, the homicide rate has decreased, but drug-related violent crimes have almost tripled over the past three years (*Houston Post,* 1987).

Increasingly, America is becoming aware of the unique ways adolescents are affected by chemical addiction. So part of the prevention question is being addressed; that is, educating the public and parents to the dangers youngsters face.

Education, however, is a strange phenomenon. Parents read these statistics every day at breakfast or see them on the evening television news. Regrettably, it is part of the human condition that knowing something intellectually does not mean understanding it emotionally. Statistics don't make an impact until your own children are in trouble–when you are parents in pain.

Long before a robbery, murder, drunk driving charge, or pregnancy occurs, mothers and fathers suspect their youngsters have a problem. In houses or apartments, in cities or suburbs, parents of all races, ethnic background, income, and educational levels worry whether their children are headed for drug abuse, trouble with the law, or the kind of dismal future that awaits the high school drop-out.

From Florida to California, New York to Texas, the parents I meet ask one question first: How can they tell when their child is in trouble? What are the signs to look for?

Over the course of nearly 13 years in adolescent treatment and five more years teaching high school in New York City, I've developed danger signs for parents to use in detecting serious drug and alcohol problems in youngsters.

Don't panic if you look at this list of danger signs and see that your teenager is showing two or three of them. For example, overreacting to criticism may just indicate your teenager is going through a hard time in English class. What you need to observe is the sum of all these parts:

1. **Changes in patterns of behavior.** A normally happy, active youngster who begins to complain, mope around, become verbally abusive, and sleep an extraordinary length of time has an unexplained change in behavior that cannot be ignored. A positive-thinking teenager does not suddenly develop a negative attitude that lasts several weeks unless chemicals are involved.

2. **Decreased interest in school and school work.** This is one of the best indicators of a drug or alcohol problem. Teenagers who normally get good marks in school and then show up with bad grades should be dealt with immediately – particularly when this happens over a short period. Sometimes students say they are bored, they don't care about school anymore, their teachers don't stimulate or motivate them. The truth is that drugs and alcohol are dulling their minds so much they cannot think.

3. **Increased irritability.** Any teenager who repeatedly overreacts with irritation and sarcasm to little things that happen at home needs some help. At the very least, he or she is a chore to live with. Teenagers – all young people – are supposed to be

happy and carefree, not negative, sarcastic, angry, and hostile. If you normally describe your youngster as easygoing, and now you have to label him as touchy and unpredictable, then you can suspect drugs, not hormones, are on the rise.

4. **Doing things for excitement that rational people would call dangerous.** Teenagers, by virtue of their belief that they are going to live forever, do reckless or dangerous things sometimes. Youngsters on drugs do things they wouldn't do normally. They tear up their neighbor's yard. They destroy their parents' property. They race trains to railroad crossings or drive on the wrong side of the interstate. They sleep with strangers and run away from home. In increasing numbers, they are riding all-terrain vehicles or dirt bikes without helmets at high speeds. They do dangerous things like these because the drugs give the illusion that they are powerful enough to prevent or survive any threats.

5. **Disinterest in appearance.** Adults and teenagers usually differ about clothes. However, teenagers who are slovenly, sloppy, dirty, and unkempt may be too affected by drugs or alcohol to see how messy they look. They may be trying to fit in with a drug-dependent crowd. This strong danger sign is one that occurs, like plummeting grades, over a relatively short period of time.

6. **Little motivation to perform tasks, and an increasing I-don't-care attitude.** This sign is most noticeable in adolescents who used to be ambitious, energetic go-getters. Youngsters who have always been laid back or lazy may be harder to diagnose with this danger signal. But parents should be alert if they often hear the words "I don't care," or if their youngster frequently shrugs his shoulders in disinterest.

7. **Money, credit cards, checks, jewelry, silver, coins, or other valuables missing and not accounted for.** No youngster should take money or anything else from a parent without permission. Chemically dependent youngsters do. In fact, they do not see anything wrong with it. Parents should realize that supporting a drug habit requires money. And chemically dependent youngsters, even in the early stages, cannot earn enough money to support an addiction mowing lawns and babysitting.

8. **Stealing outside the family.** Shoplifting is the most common form of stealing. Unfortunately, it has become almost a badge of honor for young people who do not feel they fit in. Young adolescents who shoplift feel it is an adventure. Even if they are caught, it satisfies their curiosity about what happens to young thieves. In either case, they become heros to their new friends in the drug culture.

9. **Drugs, money, clothes, albums, tapes, or stereo equipment show up at the house unexplained.** Teenagers who are supporting a habit may be earning a little extra money by providing a safe hiding place for stolen property. If your teenager cannot explain where he obtained these expensive items, he is in serious trouble.

10. **Taste in friends, music, room decorations, and clothes takes a turn for the worst.** Teenagers who are using drugs don't want to be associated with those who don't. Drugs are like a new hobby. Youngsters trying drugs or using them regularly want everything in their lives to reflect their new interest, so they hang up posters and pictures glorifying drugs or the alternative life-styles. They wear clothes that have drug culture slogans or pictures on them. Their music now features the thundering drums and destructive lyrics of heavy metal, and their musician-heroes sing of the dark side of life.

11. **Preoccupation with the occult.** Teenagers see the occult as a source of strength and power that matches the dark inner rush they get from drugs. Satan, devils, the sinister side of the occult have become the "mascots" of the teen drug culture.

12. **Physical problems such as pale face, red eyes, dilated pupils, staggering walk, slurred speech.** Parents who observe these symptoms in their children should get them to a doctor. They are either ill or on drugs. No other explanations. Teenagers on drugs or alcohol also will use heavy perfume or cologne, eye washes, mouthwashes, and chew a lot of heavily scented gum to cover the odor or effect of their drug.

13. **Irrational, explosive episodes.** A boy punches a hole in a kitchen wall when he's denied the car keys. A girl pushes her younger sister to the ground when the child won't get out of her way. A boy disciplined for breaking a rule runs up to his

room and slams the door. Of those three teenagers, only the door-slammer is normal. The other two are behaving irrationally and out of proportion to an event. Adolescents who are coming down from a drug high, where things are very mellow, are rudely awakened by how irritating real life is. That's why they are likely to erupt at illogical times.

**14. Parents, especially mothers, think of their youngsters with confusion, hurt, shame, guilt and panic.** This symptom of trouble often is ignored or attributed to the normal state of affairs for parents of teenagers today. That is a serious misconception. Children of any age are supposed to bring pleasure and joy to their parents.

The total picture presented by these 14 danger signs is that something terrible is wrong with your child. Perhaps he is not heavily involved in the sex, drugs, or alcohol of the chemically dependent world. Even if he is not, you as a parent must act quickly and decisively to get control of the situation. Just like cancer, pneumonia, or strep throat, the drug or alcohol sickness will only get worse without treatment.

Most caring, concerned, and intelligent parents today don't want to admit their child is afflicted by that most horrible of diseases – chemical addiction. They will be able to come up with a dozen explanations for the child's behavior and their own feelings of helplessness.

So those who read these 14 danger signs and still have lingering doubts about their child should apply the simple test, developed by those involved in Alcoholics Anonymous. This test grew out of the experience of thousands of recovering alcoholics: "If you think you have a drinking problem, you do." In the case of teenagers, the question becomes a statement: If parents wonder whether their child is involved with drugs or alcohol, he is.

When parents of troubled youngsters cast about for help, they discover that pastors, social workers, counselors, psychologists, their friends – even their own parents – blame the mother and father for the children's addiction. In fact, forcing parents to live with guilt has been a major obstacle to teenage recovery. Conveying blame to parents who are soul-sick from pain and worry is the biggest stumbling block for psychiatrists who seek to help parents with troubled youngsters (Robinson, 1987).

Few counseling professionals "and no one in society at large" seem prepared to help parents feel confident and self-assured in dealing with youngsters. And fewer professionals still are prepared to do anything about developing self-esteem and power in the primary care-giver, mother.

Without a strong, confident mother, any teenager is at risk for chemical abuse, and, without her, recovery ultimately will fail. Yet mother continues to be the most maligned, abused, defeated, and underrated partner in teenage drug prevention and treatment. This is not surprising since society continually sends messages to women – and to their impressionable offspring – that females, especially mothers, are not as powerful as males.

Power is the answer to questions I'm constantly asked about why youngsters resort to chemical abuse and dangerous behaviors. The youngsters are seeking power. And for every teenager on drugs there are parents who are not only in pain and guilt-ridden but powerless in their own homes. These parents inadvertently have allowed their youngsters to assume command over their lives, their homes, and their pocketbooks. It is an insidious process, which builds through time until an adolescent – the same person comedian Bill Cosby rightfully terms "brain-damaged" – is in charge of the household.

Parents then must assume their rightful places as heads of the household. This may sound easier-said-than-done. However, it is just common sense. In the final analysis, power belongs to the mentally and spiritually strongest, the person most able to use it for the greater good. That certainly lets out a 14-year-old with a Mohawk haircut who can't find his own room without assistance.

Exercising power for the greater good means making some hard decisions for a youngster who is too immature or too disrupted by chemicals to make these decisions for himself. And one of these decisions involves the music a child is permitted to hear.

Music, freedom of expression, is one of those issues that needs to be treated carefully. It is clear that overtly pornographic material needs some type of regulation, but who is to judge? The American government has no business banning or restricting any kind of music or literature. Parents, however, need to (U.S.

Senate subcommittee hearing, September 1985).

A dangerous connection exists among drugs, alcohol, sex, and certain types of heavy metal music. However, just because some types of music offend the adult ear does not mean the music is bad or harmful to youngsters. Parents need to be educated to what is on the airwaves and the cassette players of America.

Most of the so-called heavy metal music of today is not the kind of hip-swinging, sweating gyrations of an Elvis Presley that horrified parents of the 1950s. And these aren't the kind of records which, when slowed to 45 rpm and heard with the auditory perception of a dolphin allegedly reward the listener with pornographic lyrics. Unfortunately, a lot of music today is about Satanism, deviant sexual practices, raw hate, and violence on a scale unimaginable to normal adults. Yet many teenagers who are busy forming their values about women, sex, and crime know all the lyrics, and they can sing them out to the beat.

Parents in pain often tell me they thought they had instilled strong positive values in their children. What these parents forget is that their children are exposed to virile influences in society that make home values a poor defense against the evil and wrong that are glamorized by the media.

What teenagers need is not a system of values but a belief in a Higher Authority – Someone or Something more powerful than parents, drugs, or peers. Teenagers need a spirituality that many of them do not get, even those who are regular at church or synagogue. Parents sometimes confuse spirituality with organized religion. They are not the same.

Whether I am in Washington, Dallas, or Miami speaking to parents, teachers, counselors, or physicians, I keep repeating that teenage drug and alcohol abuse is about power. The cause of the problem is a youngster's search for personal power. The contributing factors are the power in drugs, sex, music, and the lack of power given to women in America. The way youngsters are rescued from chemicals is through the Higher Power and the parental power to love.

## Chapter One

Fowler, R.C., Rich, C.L., Young, D., et al. Suicide Study II: Substance Abuse in Young Cases, Archives of General Psychiatry, Vol. 43, No. 10, October 1986.

Houston *Post,* "Drug related deaths in Houston increase," June 18, 1987, as reported in Drug Abuse Update, No. 23, From Families in Action. Decatur, Georgia, Dec. 8, 1987.

Record Labeling, Hearing before Committee on Commerce, Science and Transportation, U.S. Senate, 99th Congress, U.S. Government Printing Office, Washington, D.C., Sept. 19, 1985.

Robinson, L. "In Defense of Parents," address to Central States Conference of American Society of Adolescent Psychiatry, Nashville, Tennessee, Nov. 14, 1987.

Washington *Post,*"Millions of Teens Disconneted from Society," Nov. 2, 1985.

*This is a 15-year-old's description of Tolkien's "Lord of the Rings," in which the forces of good and evil battle over the ring because of the power it contains. Just as the ring turns its owner from good to evil, so do drugs change personality and values.*

# CHAPTER TWO
# The Power to Mother

ATHLETIC, GOOD-NATURED MONICA WAS AN ALCOHOLIC AT AGE 15. She would drink and tell herself, "Look, Mom. Look at your little angel. I'm drunk on my ass, and there's nothing you can do about it."

Most mothers have no idea of the kind of power they have. In particular, they do not understand the full impact they have on their children's lives. On the contrary, most women behave as if they were important only in relationship to a man – their father, their boss, or their husband. Yet there is no doubt in a child's mind who is – or must be – the dominant force in their lives. Monica knew it even in a drunken stupor: Mother.

Adolescence is a stage in which there is re-creation of the child's earlier need to separate from mother (Blos, 1967). Mother's importance to early childhood development has been validated by many psychoanalysts (Freud, 1958; Mahler, 1975; Masterson, 1972; Masterson and Rinsley, 1975).

But what about adolescents? In the examination of disturbed adolescents and their views of parenting, it is possible to understand more about normal mothering of that age group. Normal adolescents need to recapture, at least briefly, a positive bond to a maternal figure. Even a delinquent youngster can gain the necessary internal strength if his or her prime object (mother) is strong and powerful. There is hope if a damaged bond can be recaptured, according to Winnicott (1958, 1973). If all else fails, treatment can provide the corrective experience if the environment takes into account the youngster's need for behavioral structure and positive spiritual direction. Even the most anti-social and delinquent adolescent can effectively change. It takes hard work, time, and lots of love.

In adolescence there is a step backwards to an earlier stage from which "I" emerges through trust between child and mother (Erickson, 1983). The healthy resolution of this stage depends on how powerful mother is in the eyes of the teenager. What appears to be lacking in troubled teenagers is the sense that mother is someone important. In fact, chemically dependent youngsters often describe their mothers as "doormats."

## Forces Weaken Mother

Unfortunately, these troubled teenagers are correct. The power of mother has been stripped away by four forces acting in concert: the submissive image society has stamped upon women; a domineering male in a woman's life; a woman's own unwillingness to use authority once she has it; and the erroneous notion that self-esteem for a woman rests in her paying job outside the home.

The image of women as depicted in the media is clear enough. Movies, records, television shows, and books portray females who play a subordinate or submissive role to male heroes. Adver-tisements blare that beauty and youth are the only worthwhile things women have to offer. After marriage, emphasis is given to the dual career or double income. Motherhood is given a lot of lip service but very little actual esteem or admiration.

Strong mothers often are criticized by their peers as being too strict, too mean, too old-fashioned. Certainly, their decisions are questioned by grandparents and often undercut by spouses. Mothers are bombarded with advice, pop psychology books, and seminars on child rearing. But none of these fountainheads of wisdom give them the support they seek. Indeed, mothers would feel stronger and deal more effectively with their children if they put their efforts into an organization that would support them as people and build them up as worthwhile human beings.

Too often, women allow their adequacy as people to depend on their relationship with a man. This is reflected in the teenage culture. The most popular girl is not the one with a great personality or outstanding grades. Rather, she is the girl with the most boyfriends or dates. In an adult situation, mother wraps up her self-worth in her husband or lover. One mother was so desperate to have a man in her life that she brushed aside her teenage daughter's tearful claims of molestation by this man. A woman who would not protect her child from that kind of abuse obviously is not very powerful. To no one's surprise, the teenage girl rejected her mother as a role model and leader. The youngster became chemically dependent and sexually promiscuous.

Most American children, however, do not have abusive or drunken fathers. They do have dominant fathers. These men are not cruel, unkind, or brutal. Rather, they are loving, kind, concerned fathers and husbands who do not realize what is happening in their homes. Some of them work very hard at being good parents. But they often make one serious mistake. They undermine mother's authority. As far as the children are concerned, there should be only one person whose decisions are final, whose opinions concerning them are always correct, and from whose punishment there is no reprieve: Mother.

In most American homes, mother's opinions and decisions are called into question – often in the gentlest and most reasonable of terms – by father, who thinks he knows best. Many times, the wishes of mother are ignored and the abilities of mother are downgraded within earshot of the children. When children are brought into this power struggle, it can only be destructive.

Fathers have valid, important roles to play in child-rearing. But they are supportive, not primary, roles. When men dominate child-rearing, their children lose. And so do mothers. The women become timid disciplinarians and uncertain decision-makers, and they eagerly turn over the reins of power in the family to their husbands. Once mother cannot be trusted to be the chief executive officer, the family falls apart.

Obviously, women who are dominated by men do not exercise authority in their homes because they don't really know what being powerful means. Mothers of decades past understood their authority over the home, and they used it. Stories handed down through the generations about tough grandmothers and marvelously feisty aunts confirm that women understood their authority over the home. So does the oft-repeated phrase of women today: "I would never have talked to my mother the way my child talks to me."

There are women, however, who understand authority but refuse to wield it at home. These women recognize power and see how it works in the business world. Yet they fail to make the connection between how they use power at work and how to use power at home. These women don't carry their managerial skills home from the office. Primarily, mothers in this category are still struggling with internal conflict over whether it is right for them to leave their children and go off into the workplace. The working mother's conflict between responsibilities at work and the need to be raising her children leads to anger, exhaustion, and feelings of inadequacy (Pollak, 1980). Unless these feelings are resolved, mother will not feel she can control anyone else's life since she has no control over her own.

What of the women who have no work outside the home, yet still fail to take up the reins of authority to guide their families? Most of these mothers see their *raison d'etre* as being caretaker rather than leader, actor rather than director, worker rather than manager. Sometimes these women have been led to believe a bossy wife and mother is unfeminine. Or occasionally they just don't think a child should have a tough mother as a role model. Frequently, they are coping with an alcoholic or drug-addicted spouse whose unpredictable behavior consumes all their energies.

Whatever their reasons for failing to seize control over their children, women have to overcome them. Strong mothers make strong children. That is the bottom line. The children of strong mothers may experiment with drugs or alcohol, but they are quickly jerked back into control by a mother who lets them know she will not tolerate this kind of behavior. This mother is most potent when she is assisted by a husband and extended family. In the absence of such rapport, the job is definitely tougher.

Those women who do have authority but do not use it set themselves up for feelings of failure and depression. These mothers direct their energies toward making their children as happy as possible. Mother lives her life through her children and mistakenly believes that in them she will find her own happiness. The child has everything done for him, he is protected from harm, and he has little or no sense of responsibility. She believes that this gives her power and control over her child, but in reality she is giving the child the power. The child ends up the biggest loser because he fails to see his mother as a Higher Power in his life. He does not respect his mother and fails to develop respect for other adult authority figures. The result is the Garfield Syndrome.

## The Garfield Syndrome

Garfield, the fat orange-and-black-striped cat created by cartoonist Jim Davis, lies wrapped up in his blanket. He peers out, sees a mouse making faces at him, blinks rapidly, then retreats into his blanket. Garfield is so extremely self-centered he's a joke. He wants what he wants when he wants it. He runs all over his owner, Jon, and treats Odie the dog like, well, a dog. Garfield hates Mondays since he is expected to function in a responsible way. He loves to be given things, and he is disrespectful, nasty, selfish, and arrogant most of the time. He is concerned only with his appearance and with stuffing his face with lasagna. Much of Garfield's popularity comes from laughing at how silly the fat cat is in his complete self-absorption. Part of what seems to make him such a comic figure is that Garfield thinks he is smart and cool when readers can see he is fat and foolish. However, things aren't so funny if the Garfield in your family is your son or daughter.

Children who act like they are the only things that matter in their parents' lives are self-centered, selfish, arrogant, and just plain bratty. They never give a thought to anyone but themselves and their own pleasure. A Garfield child never calls to say he'll be late coming home, since mother might say, "Come home now." She demands expensive designer jeans like her friends wear, even if she knows money is tight at home. He may refuse to sing in the church choir, even though he knows it would please his father; or, he asks to go to a movie on Mother's Day, then screams when the request is denied. The Garfield child has never known frustration and doesn't know how to handle it when he meets it, especially in the world outside his immediate family. Inside the family, he is demanding and his expectations are met – primarily to keep peace. Many analysts have commented generally on the self-centeredness of adolescents called Narcissism (Blos, 1962; Deutsch, 1944; Jacobson, 1964). More recent psychoanalytic thinking called "self" psychology describes a normal child developing away from self-centeredness into self-esteem (Kohut, 1971, 1977). Put another way, selfish children do not have positive self-esteem, nor do they learn to feel good about themselves.

## Handling Frustration

If a child gets his own way most of the time, he will discover as he grows older that he has little experience in one of life's most distressing emotions: frustration. When mother confuses the line between "wants" and "needs," she robs her child of the opportunity to learn to tolerate frustration and control his impulses. A child who cannot deal with frustration is going to put himself in situations where he doesn't have to tolerate it – a chemically induced fantasy world is one such place. In other cases he chooses the easiest way out of anything and refuses to try anything new. He resists challenges and evades experiences that offer creative growth. For example, a preteen girl who knows she is the boss at home but not at church will resist going to church camp with her youth group.

When he is very young, a child only wants satisfaction and gratification in small things: Give him a bottle and he stops crying. Later, in adolescence, he wants a truck, a car, a stereo. Give him what he wants and peace reigns. Cross him and life is a nightmare. Family relationships become a confidence game: The youngster promises to perform better in school or be nicer to siblings in exchange for privileges, clothes, a motorcycle. After parents give in, the teenager doesn't follow through with his end of the bargain. Affluence and the inappropriate handling of materialism in the family can be seen as a contributing factor to the drug abuse problem.

A child accustomed to this indulgence in material things is obsessed with controlling people. First he wants to control his parents, especially mother. When he cannot – and even the most permissive parent draws the line occasionally – the child resents the parent. These resentments are the result of thwarted efforts to control others by an individual who cannot handle frustration or anxiety. Paul, a handsome teenager recently hospitalized for abusive, aggressive behavior, was a male model for some local newspaper advertisements. He was obsessed with his body and proclaimed that his role-model was the Greek god Apollo. His mother adored him even though he abused her verbally. In the hospital, Paul was unable to get the special treatment he was used to getting at home. So he trashed his room and had to be placed in restraints.

When a youngster resents his parents for not satisfying his wants, he mouths off to them, disobeys the rules, and feels free to lie or steal from both of them, but especially mother. A youngster full of resentment may take out his anger on younger brothers and sisters, smaller children in the neighborhood, or even on pets. For example, the mother of Mike, a middle son whose unruly behavior eventually led him to drug abuse, used to get reports of her son being a bully. When control is all-important to a child, he feels a growing resentment at any frustration of his will, and that angry, bitter feeling has to come out somewhere. Generally, it shows up against those physically weaker than he. One young man used to behave fairly well when his father was at home. But when his father was away on business, the teenager punched his younger sister and pushed his mother when she tried to discipline him. When this kind of aggression and acting out occurs, the parents have lost control of the adolescent and the family unit as such is destroyed.

A child who is the center of attention – albeit negative attention – at home will be shocked to discover the rest of society doesn't subscribe to his theory of world dominance. He reacts to this disquieting information with a threatening, aggressive manner or a false, ingratiating attitude. The goal in either case is to have adults give him what he wants. There is no respect for adults in authority, no concern for the feelings of his family, and no regard for grown-ups. All adults, whether teachers, doctors, ministers, or police, are just people to be manipulated.

When a youngster sees adults in authority as people to be used, it is certain that child is self-centered, feels very powerful, and is, therefore, out of control. And there is one more certainty: His mother is unhappy and insecure. She probably is dominated by the men in her life, suffering from society's low opinion of women, and frustrated by her powerlessness at home. Although her child is only the secondary cause of her unhappiness and distress, she probably verbalizes her frustration in terms of how she can't make her teenager obey her or perform in school to her satisfaction. In fact, her unhappiness is of long standing and frequently can be traced back to her marriage or even her parents' marriage. Whatever the cause, mother is powerless, the child has become a tyrranical Garfield, and the family is in distress.

The importance of mother's role with children should not be construed as a call for women to abandon the workplace and return to the home. Instead, it is almost the opposite. Often, the best mothers are those with high-level executive responsibility in business who have resolved their own conflicts about child-rearing. These executive women are full of confidence and self-esteem, which is confirmed in the workplace as it should be at home. When these women give orders at work, they expect those instructions will be followed. Executive mothers carry this expectation home with them. Their children, like employees who want to keep their jobs, do not disappoint the boss. There is no doubt children would be better off if their mothers attended personnel management classes rather than most child-rearing courses.

If mothers must regain supreme authority over their children, it is clear fathers need to help them. Women are fighting an uphill battle against the submissive role society has mapped out for them, the naturally dominant tendencies of men, and the wish of many women to have someone – anyone – make the hard decisions for them. What fathers can do is take a hard look at their own role in child care and marriage. They must realize that, if they wish to have an influence over their children, they have to start by shoring up their wives' self-image and helping them to gain authority in their children's eyes. Some men labor under the illusion that their masculinity hangs on whether their wives agree with them on such questions as slumber parties for children, a curfew hour, or the amount of makeup a teenager can use. Fathers who feel they must win arguments when the children are around should be warned that they are loading a gun pointed at their children's hearts.

In dealing with more than a thousand mentally disturbed and

chemically dependent teenagers over the last 10 years, I have seen a distinct pattern emerge. A strong, forceful father is viewed by the children as being a bully from whom they need to be protected. On the other hand, a strong, forceful mother is viewed as a power source and a comfort to her offspring.

## Chapter Two

Blos, P. "The Second Individuation Process of Adolescence," Psychoanalytic Study of the Child, 1967.

Blos, P. On Adolescence, Free Press, New York, 1971.

Deutsche, H. "Psychology of Women," Vol. 1, Grune and Stratton, New York, 1944.

Erikson, E. "Reflections," Adolescent Psychiatry, Vol. XI, edited by Sugar, M., University of Chicago Press, Chicago, 1983.

Freud, A. "Adolescence," Psychoanalytic Study of the Child, 1958.

Glenn, S.H. "Affluence and the Family." Focus on the Family magazine, Published by U.S. Journal of Drug and Alcohol Dependence, Pompano Beach, Florida, September/October, 1986.

Jacobsen, E. The Self and Object World, International University Press, New York, 1964.

Kohlberg, L. The Philosophy of Moral Development, Harper & Row, San Francisco, 1981.

Kohut, H. The Restoration of the Self, International University Press, New York, 1977.

Kohut, H. The Analysis of the Self, International University Press, New York, 1971.

Lewis, C.S. The Lion, the Witch and the Wardrobe, MacMillan Company, New York, 1950.

Masterson, J. Treatment of the Borderline Adolescent: A Developmental Approach, John Wiley and Sons, New York, 1972.

Masterson, J., and Rinsley, D.B. "The Borderline Syndrome: The Role of Mother in the Genesis and Psychic Structure of the Borderline Personality," International Journal of Psychoanalysis, 86, 163, 1975.

Pollak, O. "Family Life and Social Change," Adolescent Psychiatry, Vol. VIII, edited by Feinstein, S., University of Chicago Press, Chicago, 1980.

Szurek, S.A., & Johnson, A. "The Genesis of Antisocial Acting Out in Children and Adolescents," Psychoanalytic Quarterly, 21, 323, 1952.

Winnecott, D.W. "The Antisocial Tendency," Collected Papers, Basic Books, New York, 1958.

Winnecott, D.W. "Delinquency as a Sign of Hope," Adolescent Psychiatry, Vol, II, edited by Feinstein, S., and Giovacchini, University of Chicago Press, Chicago, 1973.

*Spiritual struggle as seen by a 17-year-old. Only through belief in a Higher Power can each David defeat the Goliath within himself.*

# CHAPTER THREE

# The Practice of Parenting

THE KEY TO GOOD PARENTING, ESPECIALLY FOR MOTHERS AND fathers of troubled youngsters, is for the adults to feel good about themselves. Mother and father must believe and act like they are happy, secure, powerful individuals. They must have a good self-image and project an air of authority to their children. Youngsters like to know someone is in charge, and they are relieved that it does not have to be them.

For single parents, self-esteem is something to be worked at. No organization or institution comes to mind as having any program to support or shore up the weakened self-image of a single parent – usually mother. She is truly on her own to develop a belief in herself that clearly says: "I am somebody! I am a very important sombody." Paradoxically, single mothers generally are some of the strongest individuals around. They have found the courage and strength to buck the tide of society, familial expectations, and their own fear of failure by saying to an unworthy mate: "I am better off without you." Such a woman should be applauded and supported, not shunned and abandoned as society tends to do with single parents.

Of course, it is easier to parent when mother has a partner. But if that partner abuses her physically or psychologically, both she and the children are far better off alone. Efforts to keep such a marriage intact are counterproductive to the mother and the children. Even in this day and age, there are women who stay with domineering husbands because they believe they are doing their children a favor. This is not true, and often it just masks the woman's fear of being on her own.

Proper parenting and nurturing of normal adolescents is possible when mother has equality in her marriage and feels like a powerful person. Equality in a marriage relationship is vital. A child who sees a healthy male/female relationship is free to imitate parts of each sex, since each wields enviable power. Parents who respect one another's intelligence and skill tend to be flexible in their roles, compatible in the values they pass on to youngsters, and open-minded in their views on disputes and how to resolve them (Lewis, 1986). Since stress generally is a temporary thing at home, children can put their attention to resolving problems among friends, at school, or on the sports field. Best of all for children, equality in a marriage brings a sense of joy in living and immense personal satisfaction to the partners. Equality is liberating for men and women and, through them, to children.

Yet equality in the marriage does not alter the fact that the children are governed by mother. Her role might be likened to that of the chief executive officer and official spokesperson of a corporation. Just as a CEO cannot possibly run a company without delegating responsibility to others, so mother cannot function without help. If she is a single parent, the responsibility of housekeeping, cooking, balancing the budget, paying taxes, or lawn care might be delegated to someone she hires. If she is married, some responsibility for the running and upkeep of the house belongs to father – especially if mother is working outside the home.

Mother and father should confer often and privately about the proper way to raise the children, the values to be put forth, and even whether a child should be allowed to go to a slumber party Friday night. But in public – that is, in front of the youngsters – these decisions should not be advanced as corporate ones. Instead they are instructions from mother. And mother's instructions, opinions, and decisions are not to be questioned by anyone.

While his is the supportive role, father's involvement in the childrearing is vital. Father provides a strong role model: The way he behaves toward his wife will dictate how sons and daughters see themselves and how they should be treated by members of the opposite sex. Father's expectations are crucial to a child's self-image, and father's opinion always will be powerful to children. Perhaps, though, a father's biggest contribution to his children's well-being is to stand against public opinion, societal practice, and his own natural inclinations, and to allow his wife to dominate the children.

Mother, then, is the pivotal parent. Overbearing fathers may inhibit the development of a child's sense of "I"; strong mothers raise healthy adults. Except for unusual circumstances, mothers have a better sense of what their children need. This instinct about their youngsters comes from a natural bonding and from the amount of time mothers have spent with the children from birth. Mothers know their children better than fathers do.

However, mothers – weak, strong, or somewhere in the middle – do not cause drug addiction or alcoholism in youngsters. Neither do overbearing fathers. Adolescents, like all other human beings with intelligence, have decisions to make, and sometimes they make the wrong choices. The blame for a teenager's addiction rests with him alone.

Yet, once he is into a chemically induced life-style, the child's bond with a strong mother is the lifeline that will jerk that wayward adolescent back into sanity.

Giving troubled youngsters a confident mother image to cling to is the first step in recovery. What this says to youngsters is simple: "You may have gotten into trouble, but I can still help you find a way out. I have not fallen, even though you have." Such support organizations as Tough Love tell parents to detach themselves from their youngsters, then reach back and help. What this means, essentially, is that parents must give the impression they are in command of themselves. This type of attitude proclaims the joy of life without chemicals and firmly states that an adult cannot be dragged into chaos by a child.

Parenting a troubled youngster begins by setting the house in order, establishing a chain of command with mother firmly in control of the child's life. Thus it is easy to see why constantly blaming mother – or father – for the child's situation is counterproductive. Blame implies weakness and mistakes. What children want are infallible, absolutely correct parents who can be counted on for protection and comfort. Parents weighed down with guilt cannot be depended upon for either.

Parents must not assume the blame for their children's addiction for another reason. A child's recovery begins when he accepts responsibility for his own actions. He cannot do this when his parents are saying his problems are partially their fault. Parents must initiate the treatment and recovery of a chemically dependent child by making it clear the youngster is the sole cause of his own isolation, addiction, or current circumstance. In the vernacular: He brought all this on himself.

Many times parents are as addicted to their children as their children are to alcohol or cocaine. These parents are codependents. They actually allow their child's out-of-control behavior to continue by protecting the youngster from its consequences. Protection implies the difficult time will end sometime soon. That is an illusion with a chemically dependent youngster. In a healthy, happy human relationship, there is a balanced give and take. Such a balance is impossible with a chemically dependent adolescent. It is all take and no give. To keep this relationship, the parent must adapt. This behavior is called "enabling."

The middle-class mother of a 16-year-old girl who was sexually promiscuous and a drug addict said, "We parents become mirror images of the person who is drug-dependent. We develop our own system of denial and delusion, we stuff our feelings, we don't talk about the problem, and we quit trusting anyone."

Enabling behavior is weak and thus is disdained by youngsters. They see it not as an act of love and concern, but as an act of helplessness. They believe their parents are unable to stop their behavior, so they lose more respect for mother and father. Teenagers in trouble do not see protection for consequences as a strength.

All parents want to protect or save their offspring from harm. Frequently, parents rescue their children because the loving mothers and fathers do not want to suffer the pain of seeing their children miserable. Unfortunately, suffering with children who err is an inescapable part of parenting. Thus, strong parents allow children to learn that first harsh lesson of physics – cause and effect – then hurt WITH the child. That is a very significant and powerful contribution to a youngster's life.

One of the consequences of a chemically dependent life-style is to be shut out of the nuclear family. Strong families do not permit abuse. In closely knit, enviable families, everyone must make a contribution or risk exclusion. By the same token, parental love for a son or daughter always will remain, but parents do not have to subject themselves to the company of someone who makes them miserable. Unless a parent has the power to withhold approval and affection, the parent will not have the child's respect. In a teenager's world, the magic formula for respect is love plus fear of losing the parent.

Once parents allow consequences to overtake their youngsters, they have a chance to establish control of the household. As stated earlier, it is extremely important for this control to rest in mother's hands. When mother is in charge and backed fully by father, the children have authority in their lives. Now parents, with mother as spokeswoman, can set limits and rules. The rules that govern society are called values. Children are not born knowing these values, and adolescents who are or have been dependent on chemicals have forgotten what they learned. They will learn or relearn values from parents who give these instructions in the absolute.

Parents should think of their children or troubled teenagers as empty crystal glasses that must be filled up with water or values. Naturally, no parent would want to put impure water into so beautiful a container. What parents fill children with are absolutes: stealing is wrong; murder is wrong; selfishness is wrong; allowing yourself to get out of control is wrong.

Too many parents try to be completely honest with their children and present all sides of a moral issue so youngsters can judge for themselves. Youngsters really do not want that. Furthermore, the child may not be at a high enough stage of moral maturity to comprehend the significance of the parental discussion on value judgment (Kohlberg, 1981). When a preteen asks his mother what she thinks of a person who lies, the correct response from mother is that such a person is dishonorable and should be avoided. That is an absolute on which an adolescent can act.

How youngsters can think and abstract determines much of how they can handle situations involving judgment. This state is called formal operations (Piaget, 1958). Research by other scientists has shown this stage is fully achieved by very few grown-ups, with most persons only partially exerting their brains enough to think through situations (Dulit, 1972). The ability to think and abstract obviously has an effect on moral development, whether it be in adults or youngsters. Kohlberg's stages are reflected in the work of Gilligan concerning relationships and moral development (Gilligan, 1982). The importance of the development of thinking styles has enormous implications in dealing with normal adolescents as well as with delinquents and those with self-centered character problems (Dulit, 1983). Thinking is determined by brain maturity and experience. Youngsters gain experience as their parents allow it. That is one reason rigid parents do not have healthy children.

What difference is there between a rigid parent and one who sets liberating limits in absolute moral terms? A rigid parent has a laundry list of rules for everything, which is never changed by time, circumstance, or any other factor. A liberating, limiting parent sets standards that youngsters must measure up to in a fashion of their own choosing.

Youngsters should be practicing and using absolute values. Rest assured, they will make their own alterations as they mature. Parents should insist a young life start out with the values society professes to admire. As an analogy, children are not taught everything about addition, subtraction, and geometry in the first grade. Rather, they are given rules, guidelines, and numerical certainties to use as building blocks for the more challenging problems that come up later.

Families that have an equal marriage partnership, shore up mother as the primary object and commander in a child's life, set limits for teenagers, and deal in absolute values have one more step to take toward parenting troubled youngsters. Mother and father must insist the child become unselfish and think of others instead of himself.

Selflessness usually is taught in the home by having children share their toys or food with others. When a child grows older, he is ready for more advanced training in selflessness. It begins by expecting each member of the family to be sensitive to others' feelings and supportive of one another's efforts. Mother and father set the example in their marriage. If all the responsibility for peace, harmony, and happiness in the home falls on parents, there is a youngster in that house who believes he is the center of the universe.

Being considerate of others in the family leads as a matter of habit to respecting people outside the home. Thus, the ego of a youngster is kept from growing out of proportion to its genuine importance. One way to discourage a child from selfish behavior is to make disobedience and inconsiderate actions unpalatable. This can be done by mother's withholding her approval or attentions and, ultimately, by withholding a privilege.

Parents must bear in mind that youngsters are looking to them for guidance, limitations, and example. This is yet another reason why parents must develop equality in their marriages, be considerate of one another, and support one another in front of the children. Single parents – primarily mothers – must not tolerate friends who depreciate them in a child's hearing, nor should they allow their children to know if their former spouse still has some type of controlling influence on the life of the family. For the sake of the children, mother cannot allow anyone to dominate her family.

### Chapter Three

Dulit, E. "Adolescent Thinking a la Piaget: The Formal Stage," Journal of Youth and Adolescence, 1, 281, 1972.

Dulit, E. "Cognitive Development in Adolescence," Clinical Update in Adolescent Psychiatry, Vol. 1, #.O6, Nassau Publications, Princton, 1983.

Gilligan, C. In a Different Voice, Harvard University Press, Carmbridge, 1982.

Inhelder, B., & Piaget, J. The Growth of Logical Thinking From Childhood to Adolescence, Basic Books, New York, 1958.

Kohlberg, L. The Philosophy of Moral Development, Harper and Row, San Francisco, 1981.

Lewis, J.M. "The Impact of Adolescent Children on Family Systems," in Adolescent Psychiatry, Vol. XIII, edited by Feinstein, S., et al., University of Chicago Press, Chicago, 1986.

*The anger and resentment of a 16-year-old male are reflected in his drawings and in his philosophy of "anarchy"—the symbol in the middle of the drawing.*

# CHAPTER FOUR

# Nature of the Problem: Family Imbalance

WHEN PARENTS IN PAIN BRING THEIR TROUBLED TEENAGER INTO A hospital, they typically argue in front of the staff and their youngster this way: "You and your stupid ideas about letting him grow and stay out later," shouts the father. "Oh, and your idea was better? Beat him every time he looked cross-eyed," yells mother. "You really are a poor excuse for a mother, you know that," concludes father.

In these exchanges the weak parent – nearly always mother – becomes more beaten down, more unsure, and more resentful of the power wielded by the stronger partner in the marriage. When this happens, the troubled teenager loses.

No adolescent respects weakness. This is true especially of youngsters who are psychologically out of focus through drug or alcohol abuse. These young people gravitate toward power. What the child can see now is the powerful parent dominating the weaker one. That is the worst kind of behavior a disturbed youngster could see modeled, yet it probably is typical of the male-female interaction he has witnessed throughout his life.

More and more, adolescent counselors are realizing that strengthening mother in her pivotal family role means she must have equality in her marriage. Such a partnership is vital for the success of a nurturing family.

Most American families live somewhere between nurturing and dysfunctional, depending on how power is distributed between husband and wife. This imbalance is most pronounced in families with rigid belief systems and families with abusive or chemically dependent fathers. Psychiatrists and psychologists are just beginning to see how the power distribution in a marriage affects a teenager's view of the world and his place in it. But one thing is clear: The more a man dominates his wife in front of a child, the more adversely affected the youngster will be.

A family in which the balance of power between mother and father is uneven lives with a continual undercurrent of stress. Often, the woman accepts male dominance in principle but cannot live with it in practice. Many times, husband and wife are not in open conflict – in fact, they may say their marriage is happy. In any event, children don't play a part in their disputes. The trouble erupts into the open when their children reach puberty. That is the time, as noted earlier, when youngsters draw away from mother, begin developing a stronger sense of "I," then feel the need for a strong bond with mother. At this stage, teenagers become a factor in the power struggle between husband and wife, and the family becomes dysfunctional (Lewis, 1986).

For youngsters, the balance-of-power issue is not just whom to seek out for an important decision or critical advice. An adolescent seeking appropriate role models will never choose to imitate the weak parent. If the weak parent is the mother, the teenager discovers his prime or love object in life is not worthy of his affection or respect. His reaction then is to reject that prime object, treat that parent badly, and act like the power source in the family: father. That is the reason most youngsters may begin their slide into trouble by talking back to their mothers but not their fathers. These youngsters are testing the kind of power play they perceive works at home. Recent research shows that parents' attitudes toward one another do affect the child's personality, and the personality affects whether he'll get into serious problems later (Kashani, 1987).

## Slight Imbalance

Most out-of-balance American families are ruled by intelligent, gentle, caring fathers. These men dominate only through the strength of their personalities or their value systems. The wives and children of these men swallow their own feelings and desires to avoid upsetting or irritating father. The more dominant the man, the more his wife will attempt to avoid any confrontation.

Mr. Martin was a highly successful modern businessman who was very proud of his accomplishments, his house, his car, his family. In fact, the Martins had everything a family could want — until daughter Patty entered her teenage years. Then life was one crisis after another.

The high-powered Mr. Martin ruled his family with the same forceful, threatening presence he used to run his business. Mrs. Martin didn't like his overly critical attitude, but he had so many other fine qualities that she overlooked it. Patty said she hated her father, and she derided her mother as a weakling. The adolescent became insensitive to her mother's feelings. Then she began treating her mother in the same dominating way as her father did. When Patty began dating, she was attracted to boys who were "mean" to her. As she grew older, her boyfriends became more abusive and domineering. By age 16, Patty was heavily into drugs.

At home, Patty was trying to emulate her father and thereby have some of his power come to her. In the world of dating, Patty was more like her mother since the dominant male/submissive female was the relationship she saw at work.

Generally speaking, a slight imbalance of power in a marriage is hard to detect. Women who are minimally submissive aren't unhappy enough with their role to jeopardize their present life-style by complaining or seeking counseling. If the children are young, these women gravitate to the youngsters for self-esteem and comfort. For example, Mrs. Martin, who saw admirable qualities in her husband to compensate for his overbearing personality, was close to Patty as a small child.

What happens when children become teenagers is a shift in the family power structure. These youngsters begin demanding a little authority for themselves. Responsible youngsters are given the power to decide on their clothes, drive a car, go places unescorted by parents. These are all conditions that parents have controlled in the past.

This change renders the minimally submissive mother even less power in the family than before, since the authorities teenagers are looking for are usually those governed by mother. Father has not released any of his critical ways, his overbearing personality, his special times for hunting, TV, football, or his season ticket to the local college games. In fact, he is proud of the fact that nothing at home can interfere with his sports viewing.

As the teenager gains power, mother is losing it. Both now are seeking additional power from the prime source in the family: father. The Martins are an example of a family where the balance of power is only slightly skewed toward father. Here's how the imbalance showed up: In discussing how to deal with Patty, Mr. Martin hailed from the old school of harsh discipline. Mrs. Martin appealed for a gentler approach and tried to reason with Patty. Mother said she understood her daughter's rebellion. This profession of understanding and the appeal to reason is a clue that mother does not feel happy with the relationship she has with her partner. No one satisfied with the status quo sympathizes with or understands someone who is trying to destroy it. Mother had become so weak that she tried placating her daughter, who is more powerful.

For many couples, the marriage inequality – and how this imbalance is expressed – becomes so pronounced that they divorce. After the separation, the child living with one parent romanticizes the other. A child with his mother idealizes his father. Even though the father may have been domineering to the point of physical abuse, the son or daughter refuses to admit father's behavior was wrong. So the child treats mother as father used to. The weak and often exhausted mother allows it to happen. For one thing, being treated badly is a habit for her. For another, her self-image is so battered she may secretly feel she deserves this treatment. The adolescent son of such a mother is consumed with power and is abusive in all relationships with girls. An adolescent girl may reject those who show her kindness and develop relationships with boys who are tougher than she is.

Dominant male/submissive female marriages fail to produce healthy families in all cases except one: when the mother genuinely accepts and enjoys the role. These cases are rare in today's world, but they do happen.

### Serious Imbalance: Parental Alcoholism or Drug Abuse

In severe cases of imbalance, father dominates mother

through child-support purse strings, alcoholic tempers, drug-related craziness, or physical abuse. Submissive women are too busy – coping with the day-to-day panic that living with an irresponsible person brings – to shield their children. When children see that mother is too weak even to protect them from harm, they reject her.

Worse yet, youngsters who grow up in a home with at least one drug or alcohol-addicted parent have an abnormal emotional development (Ackerman, 1979). These children have become codependents. Codependency has become a buzzword in the chemical treatment field. At first the term was used only to describe the adult relatives of the alcoholic or drug addict. Now it encompasses all family members who have endured and adjusted to the destructive behavior of alcoholic or chemically dependent family members (Wegscheider-Cruse, 1985).

As the adult alcoholic slowly deteriorates, family members learn to cope by covering up for him. These coping skills may serve the youngster well at home, but they do not in society. The adult alcoholic may be losing everything from his job to his self-respect, but at home he comes across as the authority figure. He may be angry, abusive, loud, or jovial – whatever he is, the family must react to his moods just to survive. Since the adult alcoholic or drug addict does not care about the needs or wants of the family, mother and children become subservient to him. Thus, an alcoholic or drug addict who is behaving abnormally becomes the power in the family, and the rest of the family reacts to him with fear and embarrassment.

Youngsters of alcoholics or drug addicts live without maternal protection and begin to view all people in authority as they do their alcoholic parent. Their first solution is to shrink back and avoid these assertive people. This adolescent is prone to help-lessness, isolation, and depression. Inside, the youngster has intense, pent-up feelings of rage at the alcoholic parent, at alcoholism, at his helpless mother, and at his living conditions.

Part of the tragedy of the codependent child is that these youngsters have lost the chance to develop a personal identity. Children of alcoholics or addicts give up the opportunity to develop their own personalities because they are too busy being the person who takes care of drunks (Black, 1982). As a result, these teenagers rely on others for information about relationships. Girls with a weak mother believe it is right and normal to be attracted to boys who mistreat them. Or girls may reject their mothers entirely and become "tough" like their abusive fathers. Sons of alcoholic men generally form possessive, albeit inferior, relationships with girls.

Since they have been robbed of the chance to develop their own personalities, codependent children adopt the personality most familiar and powerful to them and adapt it to their use. Unfortunately, this may mean the alcoholic or addicted adult in their homes. Without knowing it or wanting it, the codependent child falls into patterns of behavior that the alcoholic parent dictates and models. Children will always gravitate to what they see as power in their homes. And the alcoholic or drug addict is the power at home (Woetitz, J., 1983). At this stage, some youngsters have education problems and may become depressed and suicidal. These are high-risk children (Deutsch, 1983). The depression in these children represents a deprivation, since early trust bonds between mother and child have not been formed (Cermak, 1986).

Many of the same factors at work in the homes of children of alcoholic or drug-addicted parents also appear with abused or neglected children. Chemically dependent adults frequently abuse their children physically and verbally.

Abusive parents show their children the destructive, negative side of power. However, children and adolescents are incapable of understanding the difference between destructive and constructive power. They understand only that this adult has authority over them and that they are afraid (Green, 1985).

Like the children of alcoholics, the offspring of abusive adults are codependents with their parents. And, like the children of chemically dependent parents, children of abusers have little self-esteem, no positive feeling about themselves, and tend to pick up the personality trait that they perceive as powerful.

## Serious Imbalance: Rigid Parents

Alcoholics and drug addicts hold their dominant roles because surviving in the family means constant adustment to the addict's twisted and erratic behavior. At the other end of the spectrum, some parents use rigid moral belief systems to establish and maintain the existing family power structure. Typical of this type of parent are career military personnel or parents who hold inflexible religious beliefs. In a very real sense, moralistic parents are as addicted to their tenets of faith and codes of conduct as the drunk is to the bottle. These parents have established escape routes for avoiding rational thought, equality with their mates, and free action.

It is characteristic of addicted or rigid parents to have difficulty understanding how their dominance or powerlessness impacts their children. While the alcoholic or drug-addicted parent has physical problems that inhibit rational thought, the moralistic parent is too self-asorbed. The partners of these domineering parents are too submissive or codependent to act independently.

Essentially, rigid parents use moralistic or religious teachings to reinforce the imbalance that exists between husband and wife. These couples gravitate toward religious institutions and organizations that seem to agree with this male-dominant belief. The inference that father's opinions are validated by God while mother's are not is a powerful weapon to use in keeping mother inferior in the eyes of her children.

The children of rigid fathers look to mother to affirm or reject this belief in a life of rules governed by father. If she submits, she is sealing herself in a tomb of powerlessness. Children do not want to identify with, or behave as, a weak adult. They might be called upon to act respectfully toward their mother, but only as father requires it. In father's absence, they will not accord mother anything but disdain. This behavior is the same as that modeled for them by father.

Just as the children of alcoholics and addicts do not have a chance to develop their own personalities, so children of rigid parents have few opportunities to learn anything but rules. Many children of inflexible parents see life not as a smorgasbord of delicious possibilities but rather as a bread-and-water diet of restrictions.

This set of rules and regulations is at war with an adolescent's effort to develop the "I" inside. Rules and religious beliefs are destructive when they restrict an adolescent rather than set him free to act within certain limitations. A 1984 survey of The

Search Institute in Minneapolis seems to confirm this. The survey of 8,000 adolescents was done for 13 youth-serving organizations, including the Baptist General Conference, the United Methodist Church, and the 4-H Extension.

The Search survey ties antisocial behavior and alcohol abuse to restrictive religion and standards set too high, which conflict with the development of independence. The survey also cites evidence that links young people from a restrictive religious philosophy to homes with coercive discipline (Search Institute, 1984).

The natural reaction of these teenagers is to toss all rules overboard. They don't want to live with the dissatisfaction they sense in their parents' lives. Besides, they can see that following the rules hasn't made their parents feel good. On the contrary, they sense mother's uneasiness and see her powerlessness to protect them. What is most apparent to these children is constant prayer for forgiveness for sins the children cannot understand or an unrelenting pressure to measure up to what commanding officer demands. The children reason—with surprising logic, in fact—that since it is impossible to meet expectations, they should enjoy themselves.

The rigid family handles crises like a slightly unbalanced one, but the mother is in more turmoil. Take the Jones Family as an example of a moralistic family. One morning, 16-year-old Marcy Jones was "not feeling like herself," as her mother later described it, but she went to school. She was a popular cheerleader but was failing in her classwork. When her mother came home from work, she noticed that Marcy was extremely agitated and weeping. She threatened to cut herself with a kitchen knife. She threatened her mother. She railed and stormed throughout the house. Finally, she locked herself in her room and refused to answer her mother's pleas.

Mr. Jones, a storekeeper, and Mrs. Jones, a bookkeeper, were active members of a church that translates passages of the Bible literally to mean that God gave men authority over women. The Joneses' joint income placed them in the upper-middle-class bracket. They had experienced a stormy marriage for the first seven years, until they obtained counseling.

Clearly, the balance of power in the Jones family was centered in the hands of Mr. Jones. This power structure was reinforced in their religious tradition, which teaches through doctrine and practice that women should play auxiliary roles in church and be submissive to their husbands at home. It was a role an accomplished woman like Mrs. Jones resented, but she had no focus for her feelings since she believed it was God's word. Her own turmoil made her relate to Marcy's rebellious feelings. She explained away Marcy's outburst by saying she had received a bad report card, which almost cost her her place on the cheerleading squad, and that her boyfriend had just broken up with her, all in a short space of time.

Mrs. Jones understood her daughter's rebellion.

## Balancing the Power

Equality in marriage and the positive self-image mother gains from such a partnership are so important in raising healthy teenagers that it is impossible to overstate it.

Equality in marriage is not intended just to unite parents on issues dealing with children. All adults who live with teenagers need to feel good about themselves as people if they are to work successfully with their youngsters. Each spouse gains self-esteem through support from his/her mate. When that source fails, the self-doubts begin. Teenagers respect strength, and adults who think highly of themselves and their role in life are strong. A mother whose opinions and contributions to family life are denigrated by her husband already has low self-esteem, or she would not tolerate such psychological abuse.

Establishing equality in a marriage is designed to make both parents happier people. Sharing the burdens of life, valuing each other as people, appreciating one another's strengths and shoring up one another's weaknesses are the bricks and mortar of happiness in any relationship. When those building blocks are off center, the entire family can crumble. And the first to feel the effects of such faulty construction are adolescents.

## Chapter Four

Ackerman, R. Children of Alcoholics, Learning Publications, Holmes Beach, Florida, 1983.

Black, C. It Will Never Happen to Me, MAC Publications, Denver, 1982.

Cermak, T. Diagnosing & Treating Co-Dependence, Johnson Institute Books, Minneapolis, 1986.

Deutsch, C. Children of Alcoholics, Understanding & Helping, Health Communications, Inc., Pompano Beach, 1983.

Green, A.H. "Children Traumatized by Physical Abuse in Post-Traumatic Stress Disorder," edited by Eth, S., & Pynoss, R., American Psychiatric Press, Washington, D.C., 1985.

Kashani, J.H.; Hoeper, E., et al. "Personality, Psychiatric Disorders and Parental Attitude Among a Community Sample of Adolescents," Journal of the American Academy of Child & Adolescent Psychiatry, Vol. 26, 6:879, November 1987.

Lewis, J.M. "The Impact of Adolescent Children on Family Systems," in Adolescent Psychiatry, Vol. XIII, edited by Feinstein, S., et al., University of Chicago Press, Chicago, 1986.

Search Institute, Young Adolescents and Their Parents, a National Research Project, Minneapolis, 1984.

Wegscheider-Cruse, S. Choice Making, Health Communications, Inc., Pompano Beach, 1985.

Woetitz, J. Adult Children of Alcoholics, Health Communications, Inc., Pompano Beach, 1983.

# ANGER COMES FROM THE INSIDE...

# ..LET IT OUT

*A 16-year-old expressed his inability to control his anger and resentment because of his drug use in this dramatic illustration.*

# CHAPTER FIVE

# The Brain and Drugs

WHEN PETITE, 14-YEAR-OLD RHONDA WAS ABLE TO UNDERSTAND where she was, she discovered she was inside the girl's detention center at Juvenile Court. She was told by a probation officer that in the last 24 hours she had snatched a purse from a middle-aged lady, tossed a brick at a church stained-glass window, and threw a punch at the arresting officer. Rhonda didn't remember any of it. Her last memory was of the party – she remembered sleeping with her boyfriend and consuming a lot of beer, marijuana and quaaludes.

Alcohol and drugs abused by teenagers disrupt normal brain development and brain function. Rhonda's blackout is only one example of how this disruption happens. In some cases, the chemical imbalance in the adolescent's head makes it impossible to judge danger. Dangerous situations are seen as exciting and fun. Other times, he has no inhibitions and shows total disregard for the consequences of his actions. Most certainly, the natural growth and maturation of the youth's brain is stunted.

## Brain Chemistry

There are several natural chemicals already at work inside the brain. These natural chemicals, called neurotransmitters, include acetylcholine, dopamine, norepinephrine, serotonin, endorphins, enkephalins, and gamma amino butyric acid. They work in different areas of the brain. Neurotransmitters make it possible for a nerve impulse to pass from one nerve cell to another like tag team relay. The main job of neurotransmitters is to relay information from one cell to another until it reaches the cell that needs the information it is carrying. An electrical impulse releases the neurotransmitter into the area between the neurons, called the synaptic cleft. The neurotransmitter then crosses into the second neuron to be stored in particular sites along the cell membrane.

When artificial chemicals like alcohol are introduced, the natural order of the brain's relay is upset. Consider these examples:

• Dopamine is a neurotransmitter that is produced in an area of the midbrain known as the substantia nigra (Fig. 1). A designer drug mistake called MPTP caused premature Parkinson's disease by destroying these dopamine-producing cells. One early theory of schizophrenia states that the disease results from an excess of dopamine, so the effectiveness of drugs used to treat schizophrenia is directly related to blocking dopamine receptors. Another extremely intriguing finding is that drugs that cause dopamine excess are the amphetamines, cocaine, and crack. Psychotic symptoms can and sometimes do result from the chronic use of these drugs.

• Norepinephrine affects the activity of the entire brain. Produced in an area called the locus ceruleus in the brainstem (Fig. 1), this neurotransmitter accelerates heart rate in reaction to stress. Together with the hormone adrenalin, produced by the adrenal glands, these chemicals control the "flight" or "fight" response of the body. Amphetamines, cocaine, and crack enhance the release of norepinephrine, leading to an excess of the neurotransmitter. This creates the "speedy" feeling.

• Serotonin is yet another neurotransmitter that has a role in mood as well as in pain tolerance and sleep. Stimulants decrease serotonin, therefore the need for sleep. LSD has a structure similar to serotonin. Narcotics increase the production of serotonin, whereas alcohol inhibits serotonin production.

• Other neurotransmitters include acetylcholine and gamma amino butyric acid (GABA). It is believed that benzodiazepine tranquilizers (Valium, Librium, Ativan, etc.) and alcohol act by increasing GABA. The effect is brain depression (Ray, 1983).

## Substance Abuse

Drug abuse is one of the nation's major problems. A 1985

household survey revealed that 113,070,000 Americans currently use alcohol, 60,280,000 use cigarettes, 18,190,000 use marijuana, and 5,750,000 use cocaine (National Household Survey on Drug Abuse, 1985).

Among high school seniors in 1986, the percentages for drug and alcohol use in the month prior to the survey were 65% for alcohol, 30% for cigarettes, 23% for marijuana, and 6% for cocaine (National Institute on Drug Abuse, 1986). Another survey showed that 5% of high school seniors drink daily and 4.9% use marijuana daily (NIDA, 1985).

The effects of drug abuse include problems with concentration, mood, motor skills, and judgment. Drugs can cause paranoia, hallucinations, and agitation. Problems with memory, attention span, and maturation cause school problems. An alarming number of accidents, homicides, and suicides are drug-related. Alcohol especially is involved in about 8,000 teenage highway fatalities annually (MacDonald, D., 1987).

Alcohol, the most popular drug among teenagers, is a central nervous system depressant. In low doses, alcohol produces excitement by depressing the reticular activating system of the brain stem (Fig. 1). This leads to cortical disinhibition and excitation by a mechanism similar to general anesthetics. The effect on the cerebellum (Fig. 5) is responsible for the lack of coordination. Judgment is decreased, and alcohol often is used prior to sexual activity because of these effects. The neurotransmitter serotonin is impaired, which may lead to an increase in aggressive behavior. Blackouts, which consist of memory loss and uncontrollable behavior, can occur during heavy drinking. Partying teenagers tend to drink like alcoholic persons – until intoxicated, or sick, or until all the alcohol is gone (Newton, 1981). This pattern of drinking leads to the development of an alcohol dependence pattern in a few short months. Adults unaware of the danger of adolescent alcohol dependence often do not consider it a problem until the alcoholism has fully developed.

Of the 1985 senior class, 66% said they drank at least once a month. This is double the number of seniors who used tobacco or marijuana and nearly 10 times the number who used cocaine during a one-month period. The problem is the pervasive prac-

Quick Facts About:

# BRAIN STEM

1. Three parts: medulla, pons, midbrain.

2. Contains reticular activating system (RAS).
Depression of RAS by alcohol or barbiturates leads to loss of control.
Arousal of RAS—creates alertness (amphetamines, cocaine, LSD).

3. Houses cranial Nerves III–XII, which control the various muscles of the face and neck.

4. Controls heartbeat, breathing, and diameter of blood vessels.

5. Rules level of consciousness/coma.

6. Neurotransmitter dopamine is depleted by designer drug MPTP.

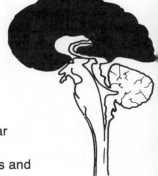

# CEREBRUM

1. Most highly evolved part of the brain. The center of intellect.

2. Motor neurons, which control movement.

3. Sensory neurons, which receive input.

4. Basal ganglia, which together with the cerebellum control movement. Rich in dopamine.

5. Contains limbic system, which oversees emotions and feelings and connects the brain to the hypothalamus. Rich in dopamine.

6. Depressed by alcohol by action on reticular activating system (RAS) in brain stem.

7. Contains the neurotransmitters endorphins and enkephalins, which are natural painkillers.

# HYPOTHALAMUS

1. Regulates heart, digestive tract, bladder.
2. Controls endocrine system.
3. Center of mind-body reactions, such as stress, panic.
4. Controls rage and aggression.
5. Controls body temperature.
6. Controls appetite.
7. Controls thirst.
8. Controls sleep through serotonin system.
9. Measures pleasure. It is most affected by cocaine.
10. Produces beta endorphins, which are nature's painkillers.

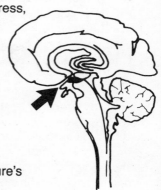

# THALAMUS

1. Acts as a relay station to the center of intellect for each of the senses except smell.
2. Contains reticular activating system, which in turn is: depressed by alcohol and causes a lack of inhibition; aroused by amphetamines, cocaine.
3. Contains endorphins or painkillers.
4. Inhibited by LSD, causing sensory overload.
5. Acts on pain and temperature sensations.

# CEREBELLUM

1. Controls movement and coordination together with the basal ganglia.
2. Disrupted by alcohol, barbiturates, methaqualone (quaalude).

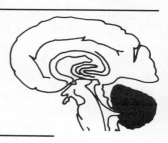

tice of heavy party drinking. This refers to the consumption of five or more drinks in a row at least once every two weeks. The rate of party drinking was highest at 41% in 1979 but levelled off at 37-39% in 1984-85. Drinking also is beginning earlier. It is estimated that 10%-25% of children will have tried alcohol by the time they are 13 (NIAAA, 1987).

## Cigarettes

Many times, a teenager's first artificial drug experience comes from a plain, over-the-counter, grown-in-America tobacco cigarette. From there, the seriousness of the chemical use escalates to alcohol, to marijuana, then cocaine. The 1985 statistics from the National Institute on Drug Abuse showed that among teenage boys, 78% who smoked cigarettes also drank alcohol. On the other hand, only 25% of the nonsmokers surveyed drank alcohol. Of those teenage boys who smoked marijuana, the survey showed 47% smoked cigarettes (MacDonald, I., 1986).

Researchers, notably men like Robert DuPont at Georgetown University, believe cigarettes are one of the earliest signs of problem behavior in youngsters, particularly those who will use "harder" drugs. When nicotine introduces the artificial chemical "high," the door is open for higher highs. The frequent use of one chemical sets the stage for use of the next chemical. Usually, the sequence is alcohol (primarily beer), cigarettes, then marijuana and cocaine – all before age 20 (DuPont, R.L., 1987).

## Marijuana

Grass, joints, smoke, maryjane, pot, hash, Acapulco gold, Columbian gold, cannabis – marijuana was the drug of the 1960s. Its sweet, pungent odor wafted around the ceilings and out the doors of many homes, dormitories, and concert halls. Not much was known about the drug then. Times have changed, and so has the grass.

When marijuana is inhaled, it produces about 2,000 chemicals. Acting on the limbic system or pleasurable sensations area of the brain (Fig. 2) in 20 to 30 seconds after inhaling, the chemicals can produce a dreamy, relaxed state in which people feel almost like they are moving through knee-high sand. Depending on the strength of the chemicals, particularly THC, in the marijuana and on the developmental stage of the user's brain, smoking grass also can produce feelings of panic and dread. The effect on the brain is similar to dementia with a loss of inhibition.

In the wonderful world of brain chemistry, the THC in grass decreases the release of acetycholine at the neuromuscular junction (Dilsaver, S.C., 1987). This dreamy state is so pleasant to chronic smokers that without the pot they are surly, angry, and irritable. The attitude problem of teenagers on pot may be due to the chronic discomfort of not being stoned. In large quantities, the marijuana affects the central nervous system. It slows things down for the youngster. The young person feels tired, moody, passive, not motivated to do much of anything in school, at home, in sports, or with family. About the only thing the chronic marijuana user thinks about is staying mellow, that is, keeping up his brain level of marijuana. This lack of motivation is an important factor in the lack of learning among thousands of high school students. It's not "cool" to work in school, especially when one is in a marijuana "I don't care" haze. This has been described as the amotivational syndrome (Schwartz, 1987).

Drug users try to sell the idea that marijuana and other types of mind-altering chemicals actually expand the mind and open it to other possibilities. That much is true. Senses are enhanced. But the ability to act on these sensations is gone. In addition, short-term recall is impaired. Although teenage users claim greater enjoyment of musical events, they often forget all the details, having been "stoned."

The Institute of Drug Abuse figures published by the University of Michigan show marijuana use has fallen off over the last few years. Daily marijuana use was down from 5% of the high school seniors interviewed in 1985 to 4% in 1987. In 1985, 26% of the seniors said they had used marijuana in the last month. In 1987, that percentage dropped to 23% (U. of Michigan, February 1987).

## Cocaine

No single drug has been given as much attention in American society as cocaine and its freebased form, crack. Until crack was developed, cocaine was a glamour drug used predominantly by celebrities. Cocaine is not physically addictive – that is, no physical symptoms or discomforts occur when cocaine levels in the body are down. The user doesn't have a runny nose or endure flu-like symptoms during withdrawal as heroin users do. Nor does the cocaine user go through D.T.'s like some alcoholics.

Then what compels people to spend $30,000 to $50,000 a year to support a chemical habit that is not addictive? The key word is psychological. Cocaine isn't physically addictive. But it is the most psychologically addictive drug on the black market. Cocaine increases the neurotransmitter dopamine, which immediately "rewards" the limbic system (Fig. 2) and the hypothalamus (Fig. 3), replacing basic instinctual drives such as hunger, thirst, and sex drive (Gold, 1987).

Cocaine zaps the pleasure center of the brain faster and stronger than any other drug. The user feels intense euphoria within several minutes of snorting the white powder, and almost immediately when the coke is "free-based" (chemically altered and smoked in a glass pipe). The drug produces such a feeling of being in control that it creates a psychological need to repeat the sensation.

Two major problems exist with cocaine. The first is money. Cocaine in the pure form still is an expensive habit to support. A gram of cocaine costs $75 to $100, and even some forms of crack can run $200 per gram. The high from coke in all its forms lasts only 10 to 30 minutes and is followed by a severe depression called a "crash." The user immediately wants another hit to attain that high. The second problem with coke or snow is that chronic use causes paranoia and increased irritability. Increasingly, police are linking irrational, irritable cocaine users with violent crimes in urban areas.

Crack is a form of freebased cocaine that is sold in pieces or "rocks." It differs from cocaine hydrochloride in that it is smoked rather than being directly inhaled. This smoking leads to euphoria in 8 to 10 seconds and lasts 5 to 15 minutes. The effect is more powerful because of absorption from the lungs to the heart and brain.

Cocaine, which is derived from the coca plant, operates on various centers of the brain to generate hyperstimulation, nervousness, and loss of appetite. The heart rate of a cocaine user during a rush can go up 50%, leading to heart arrythmia and sudden death even in professional athletes in excellent physical condition.

The National Institute on Drug Abuse showed that 17% of graduating high school seniors in 1987 had tried cocaine, and 13% had used it during the past year. Coke now is the second most-used illicit drug among high school seniors.

## Amphetamines

Black beauties, bennies, uppers, crystal, dexies, speed – all these street names describe amphetamines, a class of drugs that includes benzadrine, desoxyn, dexadrine, and biphetamine. Parents who recognize these pharmaceutical names probably have used one or more as diet aids. These drugs enhance the release of the neurotransmitter norephorine and stimulate receptors in the brain to hold some neurotransmitters while attracting others. What this means is that a child has so much energy he feels omnipotent. He is able to concentrate for long periods of time. On the other hand, he is talkative, agitated, nervous. He loses his appetite, thanks to the drug's influence over his hypothalmic feeding center; can't sleep, primarily because the recticular formation is so worked up; and sometimes he has diarrhea from the drug's reaction on his gastrointestinal smooth muscles.

Among teenagers, amphetamines are pills to be swallowed, but the drug can be taken intravenously. Taken by the vein, the drug can cause death by stroke or heart failure. Even among occasional users, headaches, depression, confusion, paranoia, cardiac palpitations, and other vasomotor disturbances can result.

In 1985, amphetamines were the third drug of choice among high school seniors interviewed by the National Institute on Drug Abuse. Girls tend to show a greater tendency to use this drug because of short-term appetite suppression leading to some weight loss. But with the introduction of new and more exciting drugs, the use of amphetamines has slacked off. However, many adolescents tend to use over-the-counter stimulants because they are cheap and legal, and because of the misconception that they are "safe" (King, 1987).

## Hallucinogens

No one who grew up in the 1960s needs much of an introduction to hallucinogens – LSD, PCP, mescaline, and peyote. The 1985 National Household Survey done under the National Institute on Drug Abuse showed that only 3.2% of teenagers had ever tried these drugs.

LSD's effects are felt in a few minutes and last up to 12 hours after the drug is swallowed in the form of tablets or squares, or chewed off paper. LSD alters brain chemistry and makes the neurotransmitters behave erratically. This produces such profound illusions as "seeing" smells and "hearing" colors, illogical thoughts, distortions of time. Flashbacks are common even without using LSD another time.

PCP, or angel dust, most often is associated with violent behavior and superhuman strength. It is cheap on the street and often is sprinkled on marijuana. Death can occur through violent acts or suicide. The drug appears to disrupt the filtering mechanism of the thalmus (Fig. 4), in the pleasure center (Luby, E., 1959).

## Narcotics

The attractiveness and availability of other illegal drugs has made heroin a drug of history and fiction for most teenagers. The National Institute's survey in 1985 showed only 1% had ever tried it. The cost is high; therefore the user has to be a criminal to get the money to pay for the drug. In addition, heroin is taken by intravenous injection.

The "rush" from heroin, which is injected, is faster than amphetamines and lasts longer. However, withdrawal symptoms begin in a few hours. Addicts need heroin several times a day to avoid being sick. Overdose is always a possibility, and death comes through pulmonary edema, suffocation, or respiratory depression. In other cases, high heroin use is connected to such respiratory problems as pneumonia, hepatitis, skin lesions, abscesses, fevers, coughs, and chest pains. In other words, heroin is a really unattractive drug – especially to youngsters. Even young teenagers today are increasingly aware that AIDS can be transmitted from intravenous drug use.

Oral narcotic drugs commonly are prescribed as pain medication for adults. Codeine is found in combination with various other medications. In addition, propoxyphene (Darvon) and oxycodone (Percodan) may be found in medicine cabinets. Drug-using teenagers may experiment with whatever they may find at home or at the homes of relatives or friends. Others, more deeply involved in drug use, may frequent emergency rooms or doctors' offices to obtain "script."

## Inhalants

In the late 1960s, there was a joke about someone being so desperate to get high that he flew with airplane glue. Of course, the joke didn't mention the brain damage such a flight caused. Most of the inhalation of such solvents as liquid paper, glue, paint thinner, freon, and gasoline is done by young adolescents, and its use decreases as the youngster grows. Only 1% of seniors had used an inhalant orally prior to the National Institute survey in 1985. Some of the attraction of these inhalants, especially amyl nitrate, is the belief that they enhance orgasms. Other inhalants depress the central nervous system and create confusion and disorientation. Young kids have died from suffocation by displacing the oxygen in the lungs (NIDA, 1983).

## Ecstasy and Eve

Ecstasy (3,4 methylenedeoxymethane amphetamine) was classified as a controlled substance or narcotic on Sept. 1, 1985, by the Drug Enforcement Administration (DEA). Prior to that, it was a legal drug since it was produced as an analog. What is most unfortunate, according to Dr. Mark Gold, cofounder of the 800-COCAINE hotline, is the attitude of street-drug users. Young people view drugs as safe until proven dangerous (Gold, M., 1985). The medical profession and the Food and Drug Administration (FDA) assume all new medicines are dangerous until proven safe.

After the criminalization of Ecstasy, the "Eve" (3,4 methylinediopyethamphetamine) appeared. Since then, the Journal of the American Medical Association has reported five deaths associated with Ecstasy and Eve (Dowling, 1987). Users report that these drugs allow them to get in touch with the "self" and enhance insight and thinking. A few psychiatrists were using these drugs with patients prior to its being made illegal.

## Designer Narcotics

Synthetic drugs have been made from the legitimate drug fentanyl citrate used in surgery. Fentanyl is 100 times stronger than morphine. One designer, 3-methyl fentanyl, or MPTP, is 2,000 times as potent as morphine with rapid onset of action. A horrible mistake occurred when MPTP was produced, which gave the user a syndrome similar to Parkinson's disease. The drug destroys the brain's substantia nigra. These drugs often are sold on the street as heroin, "china white," or "zoom" (JAMA, December 1986).

The good news from the NIDA survey done by the University of Michigan is that abuse of all these drugs among high school seniors appears to be on the decline. The bad news is that the researchers did not interview the 28% of incoming freshmen who drop out of high school before their senior year. Other studies indicate these drop-outs have serious drug or alcohol problems that contribute to if not directly causing a decision to leave school. The National Institute survey shows 61% of high school seniors used illicit drugs in 1985 compared to 58% in 1986. But this news is cold comfort indeed if your child is a statistic (U. of Michigan, February 1987).

### Chapter Five

Dilsaver, S.C. "The Pathologies of Substance Abuse and Affective Disorders," J. Clin. Psychopharmacology, Vol. 7, No. 1, February 1987.

Dowling, G.P.; McDonough III, E.T.; and Bost, R.O. "Eve and Ecstasy – A Report of 5 Deaths Associated with the Use of MDEA and MDMA, Journal of the American Medical Association, Vol. 257, No. 12, March 27, 1987.

Dupont, Robert L. "Prevention of Adolescent Chemical Dependency," Pediatric Clinics of North America, Vol. 34, No. 2, 495, April 1987.

Gold, M. "Ecstasy, Etc.," *Alcoholism and Addiction* Magazine, September/October 1985.

Gold, M. "Crack Abuse: Its Implications and Outcomes," Resident and Staff Physician, Vol. 35, No. 8, 45, July 1987.

King, P., and Coleman, J.H. "Stimulants and Narcotic Drugs," Pediatric Clinics of North America, Vol. 34, No. 2, 349, April 1987.

Luby, E. "Study of a New Schizophrenomimetric Drug-Sernyl," AMA Archives of Neurology and Psychiatry, 81, 113, March 1959.

MacDonald, D.I. "How You Can Prevent Teenage Alcoholism," Contemporary Pediatrics, Vol. 50, November 1986.

MacDonald, D.I. "Patterns of Alcohol and Drug Use Among Adolescents," Pediatric Clinics of North America, Vol. 34, No. 2, April 1987.

Medical News, "A Growing Industry and Menace: Makeshift Laboratory's Designer Drugs," JAMA, Vol. 256, No. 122, Jan. 12, 1986.

National Clearing House for Alcohol Information "Alcohol and Youth," MS 333, January 1987.

National Household Survey on Drug Abuse, 1985, printed in Drug Abuse Update, from Families in Action, Decatur, Georgia, No. 19, December 1986.

National Institute on Drug Abuse, 1985, printed in Drug Abuse Update, from Families in Action, Decatur, Georgia, No. 16, March 1986.

National Institute on Drug Abuse, 1986, printed in Drug Abuse Update, from Families in Action, Decatur, Georgia, No. 21, June 1987.

National Institute on Drug Abuse, "Inhalants," DHHS publication No. 83, 1307, 1983.

Newton, M. "Gone Way Down," American Studies Press, Tampa, 1981.

Ray, O. "Drugs, Society and Human Behavior," C.V. Mosby Co., St. Louis, 1983.

Robinson, T.M.; Killen, J.D.; et al. "Perspectives on Adolescent Substance Use," JAMA, Vol. 258, No. 15, 50, Oct. 16, 1987.

Schwartz, R.H. "Marijuana: An Overview," Pediatric Clinics of North America, Vol. 34, No. 2, 305, April 1987.

University of Michigan, ISR Drug Study, News and Information Services, Feb. 10, 1987.

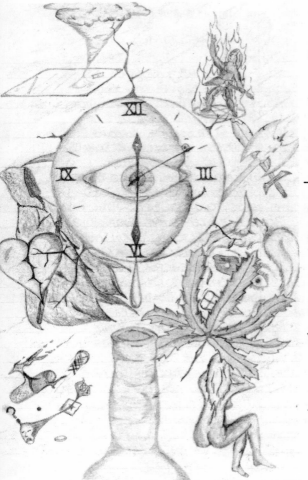

## NIGHT TIME CRIES

NIGHT TIME CRIES AS
IT SEES THE UNDOING OF
THE DWELLERS OF THE
NIGHT TIME WORLD...
—A BOTTLE OF SORROW
DRIES OUT ALL
YOUR DREAMS—
—THE LEAF SO SWEET
BLINDS THE MAN FROM
THE BEAST—
—SWALLOW A PEARL AND
LOSE TOUCH,
QUESTION THE WORLD—
—BREATHE THE DUST,
IT RISES TO A STORM AND
BLOWS YOU AWAY—
—HUNGER FOR LUST—
—HUNGER FOR BLOOD
YOU LIVE ONE A BLADE:
DANCE ON THE EDGE—
—PLAY WITH FIRE
YOU BURN YOUR FINGERS
AND LOSE YOUR HOLD
ON THE FLAME—
—YOUR LIFE BEATS
ON A BROKEN HEART—
—CAN'T YOU SEE YOU'RE
GIVING DEATH A KISS?—

—SOMEONE
WHO MADE
IT

*Feelings of fear, chaos, and power are all evidenced in this drawing done by a 15-year-old.*

## CHAPTER SIX

# Nature of the Problem: Alcohol, Cigarettes, Sex, and Cars

DORIS WAS RATHER PLAIN. BUT SHE WAS A SWEET 15-YEAR-OLD with that wholesome look of country living and a solid family life based on love, caring, and sharing. Her grades were good, and she played in the school band. But Doris wanted boys to like her. So she painted on makeup and "perm'd" her hair. Next, she started hanging on the fringes of a tough crowd. She took up smoking, drinking alcohol, and sex. She had as many dates as she could handle. She belonged. She was popular.

Whether your teenager is lying, stealing, cruising with the family car, or dabbling with sex or cigarettes, the underlying goal is to feel grown up. As parents, you may take it as one of few certainties in this life that children lie, steal, do drugs, and drink alcohol to feel more confident about themselves – even if only temporarily.

There are some very good scientific reasons why bad grades, erratic behavior, and the rest of the unlucky 13 danger signs mentioned in the first chapter point to alcohol and drug abuse. For now, just remember that alcohol and drugs change behavior because they are mind-altering. Mind-*blowing*, the teenagers very appropriately call it. What a young person would never do while in his right mind he will do while his mind is chemically altered. Adult social drinkers who have ever had too much to drink at a party and awakened the next day with a lampshade on the bedpost can understand how this scenario works.

The difference, of course, is how the adult and teenager

arrived at their hangovers. The adult may have slipped into his accidentally – perhaps by not paying attention to how often the host filled his glass. In contrast, the partying teenager takes that first gulp of beer with the express purpose of getting drunk. Adult social drinkers drink alcoholic beverages to be sociable and because they like the taste. Teenagers drink to get drunk. And they get drunk to feel powerful and grown up.

## Alcohol Power

Adolescents – and with the earlier onset of puberty, that means everyone from 10 to 18 – drink alcohol to feel powerful and in control. At rock bottom, that is the reason it all begins. When he's high, a skinny, pimple-plagued boy becomes as handsome as Robert Redford. An overweight girl with kinky, curly hair becomes as gorgeous as Cybil Shepard. A young man who can't slam-dunk a wad of paper into a wastecan becomes the fabulous Dr. J., or a slow student becomes a scientist like Marie Curie without study, practice, or effort.

In reality, very few people are as glamorous as Robert Redford and Cybil Shepard without working out a lot and submitting to an hour's makeup session before the cameras roll. But reality doesn't mean anything to a teenager who has experienced how good life can be on a high. The youngster *feels* strong, handsome, and smart. He *feels* powerful. He has people looking up to him. His parents are racing around like crazy protecting him, explaining away his behavior, getting him out of trouble. He is the center of the universe. Besides that, life on a high seems very pleasant. It's only the coming down that's no fun.

Once a youngster has tasted life on a high, life without it is twice as difficult. Alcohol is attractive to youngsters from all socioeconomic, religious, and moral backgrounds because every teenager shares the same insecurities about his own worth. Besides, alcohol is legal for adults. Even a youngster to whom adults would point as having good looks, a quick mind, material advantages, and a bright future may feel inadequate. That's what all those raging hormones do for adolescents. How anyone survives to adulthood is one of nature's great miracles. Yet over the centuries, millions of people have traversed this thorny ground relatively unscarred.

With rare exceptions, teenagers feel stupid, weak, uncertain, awkward, and not very pretty (or handsome). They look around and wish they had prettier hair, nicer clothes, better grades, cuter boyfriends (girlfriends), clearer skin. These youngsters see there are older people in the world who are always cuter, smarter, cooler, sophisticated, and in command. They see too that some people their age seem cuter, smarter, cooler, etc. They want to imitate grown-ups without accepting the responsibilities of adulthood.

Adults esteemed by teenagers are television heroes, movie stars, rock singers, older young people – anyone who is in control, confident, doesn't take any lip from the boss, and lives dangerously. These are glamorous people whom teenagers never get to see when they have a bad day or stub their toes. No teenager ever gets to see Tom Cruise sick as a dog with a stomach virus. But the adolescent sees moms and dads wash clothes and spend the day moaning with stomach cramps. These media-made heroes and heroines are tough, bad and – most important – cool.

## Being Cool

There is no way to stress how important it is for a teenager to be cool. And in with a group. Youngsters are very susceptible to peer pressure. They want to belong to something. In the 1940s and 1950s, it used to be enough for most youngsters to belong to a school and sing the fight song until they were hoarse. In the 1960s, it wasn't cool to be cheerleaders or football captains; they had to be rebels. In the 1970s, there was a move to preppies, sororities, and self-centered small groups – perhaps as a reaction to the increased computerization in their lives. Today, there are the untouchable punk rockers, head-bangers, and the disenchanted, the burn-outs.

While it is true that every teenager wants to be admired and in with a group of young people, most youngsters find other activities to occupy their time. They don't spend all their time being cool. They may have best friends, but they don't shun everyone else in the world. They may like rock music, but they don't live and breathe it. In other words, there is some balance in their lives.

It may seem to you that your daughter spends hours grooming herself, selecting just the right oversized shirt to wear with that small skirt and talks of nothing but how terrific musician Steve Winwood is. But, when you stop to think about it, she has other interests. Doesn't she ride bicycles, play on the soccer team, swim, argue with the debate club?

A child headed for trouble is preoccupied with "being cool." Everything he or she does is pointed toward an appearance of self-assurance. Therefore, if it is not cool to go swimming, your child will sweat and stay dry even if swimming once was his favorite pastime. Unfortunately, being cool is a lot more than just *appearing* confident and "bad."

Looking cool boils down to imitating adults. An adult has power and control. Adults do whatever they want, or so it seems to teenagers. A young person who does whatever he wants appears as powerful as an adult. Other teenagers look up to this supposedly mature teenager. The more things a teenager can do that only adults are supposed to do, the more grown-up he is. Life would be easy if teenagers wanted to imitate the responsible, hard-working, dependable side of adult living. Unfortunately, too many teenagers see adults as beer-swilling, cigarette-smoking, love-making creatures bent on personal gratification.

Youngsters know that when they drink beer, smoke cigarettes, and have sex, adults don't approve. Adults alone may do these things. Therefore, teenagers rationalize that drinking, smoking, and intercourse must be the rites of passage from childhood to adulthood – acts that transform children to grown-ups and admit a young person to that most powerful of estates – adulthood.

Generally, an inappropriate search for maturity begins with a regular tobacco cigarette. In most states, cigarettes are illegal for anyone under 18. This little nicety is glossed over by teenagers since they really have no concept of legal and illegal. Neither, apparently, do those high schools that provide smoking areas for students – although most teenagers in high school are under 18. A study reported in the New England Journal of Medicine showed that drivers who smoke are a high-risk population to be charged with drunk driving. The reason cited is that smokers are risk takers, and this is reflected in their driving (Winters, T.H., 1985).

The youngster with a cigarette, perhaps visualizing himself as the Marlboro man, is doing something adult. His artificial confidence exudes power – he is cool. Other teenagers may react to his false sense of self-worth and look at him with a new respect. These other youngsters say he's cool. He must have some power over adults, or they would stop him from smoking. The "cool" youngster himself is having some very powerful thoughts about the adult reaction to his smoking. Adults can't or won't stop him. Now he is also a little scared. Adults can't or won't stop him, and he knows he isn't always in control. Who is, then?

The next negative behavior that seems to follow cigarettes is drinking alcohol, primarily beer. Linda, a painfully shy 13-year-old, found confidence in a bottle. At the time, it seemed like a perfectly acceptable way of handling her acute shyness, she said. Everyone drank at school dances and parties. She fit in when she drank. Later, she discovered, not allowing her self-confidence to develop naturally paved the way for her cocaine habit.

Teenagers usually have seen their parents and other adults drinking. And they probably have seen college students laughing and acting silly – having fun – while they drank alcohol. So they know drinking is the socially accepted thing to do. This is true especially with beer for a number of reasons. Beer is American. Beer is sold in grocery stores in most states right near the peanuts and soda pop. Beer is football, baseball, basketball. You think not? Just watch television and see what's advertised during these games, and who's doing the commercials. The way television portrays it, beer is right up there with motherhood and apple pie. Certainly, it is the thing to drink if you are an adult.

Follow an insecure teenager's thinking to the next step: If it is cool to smoke cigarettes and drink alcohol like adults the youngster admires, it also must be cool to engage in sex like adults do. Using their sexual organs the way adults do makes a teenager feel powerful – and it is fun. Sex is something only adults are physically able to do. For a boy, sex is a physical power over someone around whom he is a little scared or nervous. For girls, having sex means popularity – boys are attracted to her. Of course, when drugs or alcohol are involved, there really is no need for an excuse. Sex seems to go with the territory. The media tend to influence teens by portraying sex as the route to popularity, glamour, and happiness. Girls for whom sex is a life priority stunt their emotional growth and settle for an "infantile personality" (Deutsch, 1967; Blos, 1980).

Naturally, teenagers don't sit down and think all this out. In the first place, their brains aren't developed enough to reason this way intentionally. And who sits down and analyzes his or her daily behavior? But it is helpful for parents to understand how the teenager views life and the "forbidden" fruits around him.

## Cars and Trucks

Among the steps to trouble is a new one made possible through modern technology and the affluence of society: the irresponsible use of motor vehicles. To most youngsters a car or sporty truck is not a mode of transportation or convenience. It is a rolling party. Those growing up in the 1950s and 1960s certainly can relate to that. Who hasn't driven the car around and around the hamburger joint, looking for cute members of the opposite sex? Cars and trucks are different for many of today's youth. The vehicles represent status, independence, and power. Combined with liquor or drugs, a machine with a motor can make a child feel invincible, beautiful, worthy of everyone's envy, and totally in command of all he surveys. Here's how important youngsters consider their wheels: A Missouri father brought his son to a counselor. While he was drunk, the boy had wrecked three trucks and currently was driving his fourth. The psychiatrist immediately told the father to take the truck away from his son for good – and the boy attacked the doctor. Later, after the boy had been subdued and became calm, he said, "When I get behind the wheel and I'm loaded, I crank up the music, step on the gas, and I got 3,000 pounds of macho machinery under me – and off I go."

Making a motor respond on command is macho. Teenagers often don't understand that it also is dangerous. In this context, "understand" means "feel." Most teenagers – particularly those who have been drinking – don't accept as a fact in their lives that abusing a motor vehicle can kill them. Yet, most can recite chapter and verse from what they've been taught about the dangers of driving recklessly. Many youngsters stop careless behavior with motor vehicles after one traffic ticket or after their parents take the dirt bike away for a specific period. Others require more persuasion from adults. However, a youngster in trouble is compelled by the invincible feeling of drugs or his need to prove his worth to repeat his dangerous conduct. Being reckless behind the wheel is considered a vital part of the confident image these youngsters must project.

As in all things, there are degrees of involvement with these steps to dependency. Some teenagers attempt to be cool with cigarettes or beer tasting, then decide it's not for them. Some may focus on sex. All find peer pressure quite intense. A 1987 Weekly Reader survey of 100,000 elementary and junior high school students showed that, at the fourth grade level, 36% report pressure to try alcohol. There also are pressures to drink wine coolers and try cocaine (*Chicago Tribune*, April 1987).

## Indestructible Teenagers

Young people don't have a concept of physical harm or death, especially in the long term. There are educational programs in schools, churches, and on television that talk about the harmful effects of cigarettes, alcohol, and promiscuous sex: lung cancer, emphysema, cirrhosis of the liver, delusions, AIDS, unwanted pregnancy. But youngsters do not think they will get pregnant, become ill, or die. They are in their physical prime. They have fewer colds, earaches, and other illnesses then when they were little. Sometimes they can't remember what it's like to feel bad! When they do get the flu or a virus, they act surprised, mystified, even insulted.

At about 10 years old, youngsters feel physically omnipotent, invulnerable, invincible – and every year they grow stronger, bigger, and more developed. So it is hard for them to imagine that they should not be smoking cigarettes because some day, in that great future beyond, they will be unable to walk without coughing, and eventually the cancer will choke off their breath altogether. Parents have to remember who they are dealing with here: These teenagers are the same people who can hardly think past getting their homework done for next week. Small wonder they can't think 20 years down the road about the effects of cigarette smoking.

This same short-sighted thinking applies when it comes to sex. Teenagers do not think of sex in terms of procreation. They think of it only as fun and power. Someone suggested that all music lyrics begin crooning about "making babies" instead of "making love" and see if the number of teenage pregnancies declines. Nice idea, but it wouldn't work because it is very rare for a child to link sex with pregnancy. Not, at least, the sex they have – or their own pregnancy. It's like a car accident – it always seems to happen to someone else.

Rarely do youngsters use or think about contraception. They know about condoms, IUDs, foam, birth control pills. Health and sex education classes in public schools are full of information about where babies come from and how to prevent pregnancy. But when the time comes to act on this information, the rule is that the younger the teenager the less likely he or she is to use contraceptives. Usually, a girl begins taking birth control pills after an abortion. The parents then are aware their daughter is sexually active, resign themselves to it, and insist that preventive measures be taken.

Among sexually active teenagers, contraception is very much the girl's responsibility. The boy doesn't feel any moral, ethical, or legal responsibility in any of it. Part of that is the macho image most young men still are required to project in this society to have any self-esteem. And the other is just a simple fact of nature. Females carry babies; males don't. A male can walk away from the problem at any time; a female takes it with her wherever she goes. A boy may promise he'll stand by his girl and may even make a stab at it. But in the end he probably will walk away.

Just as teenagers don't see the long-term effects of cigarette smoking or sex without protection, so they don't understand the consequences of drinking. Youngsters don't see any harm in being drunk, unless you count the minor inconvenience of a hangover. Even a hangover is a badge of honor. Teenagers see drinking as fun, their drunken behavior as an expression of fun.

In fact, the more drunk they get, the more out of control they behave, the more they pass out or throw up, the more cool they believe they are. They try to drink more than anyone else because drinking capacity is a measure of their maturity. They don't care about the unhealthy consequences of drinking themselves into a stupor. Nor do most of them care about drinking and driving. Again, car accidents happen to someone else. Besides, they see alcoholics as old, fat, sloppy. How could someone young, trim, and good-looking be an alcoholic?

In short, teenagers don't see the consequences of their actions. They don't feel danger looming over irresponsible behavior. They don't understand how time and the forces of nature speeded up by abuse can deteriorate the human body. They've experienced only how nature makes a body grow stronger.

Children also don't see the underneath side of every pleasure. Teenagers see the glamorous rock star, but they don't see the hours of make-up that go into being beautiful and the years of practice needed to make music. Youngsters see adults enjoy liquor, but they don't see liquor as fun in moderation. Adolescents find sex a thrill, but they don't see the connection between the pleasure and a screaming infant with smelly diapers or a retching pain in the gut from an abortion.

They will not understand danger and be able to act on this understanding until their brains are more fully developed. The parents' goal is to keep them from learning these lessons the hard way – by experience.

## Love in the Drug World

Even without drugs, young people often are involved in intense relationships they call love. When a teenager is around his true love, there is a charged atmosphere. At home, he moons and spends hours on the telephone. A girl in love may lose her appetite and devote lots of time to romantic songs and even poetry. Young people are so consumed with one another that their school or work habits suffer, and even family relationships take a back seat. It's a familiar scene to most parents.

In reality, young people aren't in love, although it is foolish to tell them otherwise. What they are experiencing is a pleasurable sensation that comes from the attention of a member of the opposite sex. Such attention is worth a lot in terms of self-image and self-worth. But when the period of excitement is over, one of the two teenagers moves on to someone else. There is a breakup that seems disastrous to the person left behind.

Adolescent relationships, as parents know, are built solely on excitement, pleasure, and stimulation, with no commitment or plans for the future. The more intense the relationship, regardless of whether the couple engages in sex, the less a teenager develops personally. Even in teenage relationships that do not involve drugs, personal growth is replaced by the pleasure principle. Fortunately, pleasure is a fleeting thing, and this enables healthy youngsters to recover from a broken romance in short order.

Actually, teenage relationships demonstrate behavior patterns similar to addiction. In many of these teenage relationships, the youngsters may use drugs together. So there is the double attraction of romance and a high.

When drugs are a part of a relationship, two things nearly always are true for a middle- to upper-middle-class girl: She is being dominated and abused by her boyfriend, and he is supplying the drugs. Exceptions to these characteristics are rare. The girl deludes herself into thinking she is "in love" because this makes sex acceptable. Love makes all things right in the teenage mind – their music, their media, and their culture seem to tell them so.

Troubled teenage girls lose the most in the drug culture. They lose their health, their self-respect, their morals and values, and control over their own bodies. They find themselves at the mercy of boys in the drug crowd, since the boys supply the drugs. The girls discover their opinions and values don't count for much. The music favored by youngsters in the drug culture may even validate sexual abuse of females.

Ironically, the troubled girl with no goals, no clear self-image, and no joy in living dominates her home through out-of-control behavior, yet she becomes a weakling in society. Girls are abusive to their mothers, whom they disdain as submissive, yet in their relationships with boys they become the abused. The tougher the girl is at home, the tougher – or older – her boyfriend is likely to be.

Even girls who grow up in families where power is balanced between mother and father go through a period of extreme vulnerability in early adolescence. These strong girls are not attracted to abusive males but are interested in boys who appear to have some "power." Often, this is in the form of fashionable clothes, good looks, money, or a car. This, as every woman will recall, is a normal part of a girl's adolescence. As she matures, a girl will begin looking beyond the exterior for something deeper.

For troubled teenagers, the boy who seems most powerful and attractive to girls generally is someone in the drug culture. The girl is drawn to his popularity with a crowd, to his "cool" exterior, and to his defiant behavior that seems to mirror her own. Whether he is mean to her, talks her down in front of friends, stands her up when they have a date, forces her to have sex, fails to call for a week, or actually hits her, the girl believes this is part of a normal male-female relationship. It is the type of relationship familiar to her. Once the romance ends, the girl sees continued drug use as the only road back to popularity.

If her mind were free of chemical alteration, the girl might stand up and reject this abuse. But nothing constructive is possible within a mind that is not hitting on all cylinders. The boyfriends dated by Tracy, an extremely good-looking teenager, were into partying – that is, loud music, fast cars, liquor, sex, and drugs. Partying gave Tracy the power to feel good about herself and to bury her guilt feelings. She rarely bought a drink or joint herself. Instead, she formed relationships with boys or men who could give her a high. In return, she gave them sex – without a moment's hesitation. The only thing she regretted was hurting her mother.

When Tracy was hospitalized for drug and alcohol dependency, she wrote, "I'm thankful I did get caught. I know my mom doesn't have to worry about where I'm at, who I'm with, and what I'm doing. She gets a chance to rest easy and take care of herself for the first time in a long time."

An insecure teenage boy with a poor opinion of himself, no concrete plan for the future, and no happiness within seems to latch onto an "image" as a way to be somebody in his world. His world is filled with demands to be athletic, talk baseball, knock somebody over on the football field, make decisions, be tough.

One convenient image for many youngsters is that of a rock star he sees on MTV or in the movies. The tougher the image, the better he feels about himself.

Now, all boys go through this macho, Mr. Kool stage to some extent. Many men will remember a time they wanted to ask a plain Jane to go out because they liked her. Instead, they opted for a miserable time with a popular girl because that would improve their image. As boys mature and find power in acceptable places, they learn that being cool, macho, and tough isn't what being a man is all about.

Drugs that turn up the heat on newly developing aggression in a boy are very attractive to him. These drugs make him feel invincible. He is powerful. At home, he has seen his father control the household, so he imitates his father. That means he must have a submissive female to abuse. He must have a girlfriend who looks up to him as a god. Such a girl makes him feel more powerful and self-centered. To ensure that he finds and keeps a girlfriend, he offers drugs. Now, his male supremacy is confirmed by stealing and dealing drugs – things his girl counts on him to do. In exchange for his largess, he expects sex. Sexual relations are part of his domination. He can't be a macho man *and* a virgin.

## Dependent vs. Independence

Josh was a handsome 16-year-old who thought he was God's gift to girls. His mother doted on him, protected him, and accepted his verbal abuse as she had accepted his father's before the U.S. Army transferred him and they divorced. To numb his feelings of insecurity and guilt at the way he treated his mother, and to give himself instant pleasure, Josh experimented with drugs. He was a natural leader and became a powerful figure in the local teenage drug culture. He then fell in love. His girlfriend idolized Josh. He depended on her to affirm his self-image. He stole from his mother and other relatives to buy drugs when his mother denied him money. At one point in his torrid romance, Josh began to feel his girlfriend loved drugs more than him. He tried to get her off chemicals – and she was so angry she tried to get back at him by taking an overdose. He became obsessed with her – so much so that even after he was hospitalized he continued to quiz visitors about her. He even gravitated to the girls in the treatment program to improve his self-image.

Note that in Josh's story the person who ended up being hurt the most by a dependent relationship was his girlfriend. In a drug scene, the female trades her body for power. In a romantic relationship that involves drugs, she relinquishes control of her self-worth as well as her body. Even without drugs, a girl who develops a dependent relationship at this juncture in her life has enrolled in a course on how to be a repressed, unhappy woman. Submission is not a natural condition in a human being — especially in an adolescent human being.

The internal conflict for a youngster who must be submissive to have what he or she desires, but who wants to be free to explore and grow, can be resolved temporarily, but spectacularly, by doing drugs. The child's personal development and growth stops at that point, even though chronological years keep piling up. Every girl's personal development stops at the submissive-passive stage when she is on drugs and having sex at her boyfriend's command.

Even boys who have been raised to be gentle, kind, caring, and law-abiding can become overly aggressive and sexually demanding when they are influenced by chemicals and in the arms of a teenage girl.

The power in drugs is the artificial rearrangement of a developing brain at a time when youngsters are most susceptible to emotions and suggestions. This rearrangement makes irrational and immoral thoughts, perceptions, feelings, and deeds appear rational, proper, and even good.

Drugs are not the miraculous cure for inadequacy that teenagers are seeking — but they are a very attractive power.

### Chapter Six

Blos. "Modification in the Traditional Psychoanalytic Theory of Female Development," in Adolescent Psychiatry, Vol. VIII, edited by Feinstein, S., University of Chicago Press, Chicago, 1980.

*Chicago Tribune*, "Peer Pressure to Drink," April 24, 1987, as reported in Drug Abuse Update, from Families in Action, Decatur, Georgia, No. 22, September 1987.

Deutsch, H. Selected problems of adolescence. Psychoanalytic Study of the Child, Monograph No. 3, International University Press, 1967.

National Institute on Drug Abuse, Twelfth Annual Survey of Drug Abuse Among High School Seniors as Reported in Drug Abuse Update, from Families in Action, Decatur, Georgia, No. 22, September 1987.

Winters, T.H. & D.; Franza, J.R. "Smoking and Drunk Driving," correspondence section, New England Journal of Medicine, 213, 1421, Nov. 28, 1985.

*Graffiti-type art done by a 14-year-old demonstrates the importance of rock 'n roll and drugs because both symbolize power.*

# CHAPTER SEVEN

# Nature of the Problem: Heavy Metal Music

LIGHTS FLASH ON AND OFF IN RAPID SUCCESSION, VARYING PAT-terns, shades of yellow, red, and white. The sound of thundering bass and the pounding drums beat against your chest like a physical assault. Performers in tight blue jeans, ragged tee shirts, and fringe vests jump and gyrate on the stage. Thousands of youngsters in the audience scream, and many try to rush the stage.

Welcome to a heavy metal concert. It is nothing like the hysteria over Elvis Presley and his hip-shaking rock and roll, or the mania that accompanied the long-haired Beatles across the Atlantic. Here is the difference: In the middle of the aisle, a teenager with "Born to Raise Hell" on his tee shirt holds aloft a paper cup and yells, "Kill! Kill!" Off to the side, a teenage girl in the row behind you is giggling madly, and you can smell beer all the way to your seat. The police will arrest dozens of youngsters ranging in age from 12 to 18 for drug and alcohol abuse. At one Motley Crue concert, almost 100 were arrested (Branston, J., Jan. 5, 1986).

The concerts and records of heavy metal musicians are cap-sulized versions of the world for disconnected, insecure young-sters. The concert and music reflects how troubled youngsters think they should feel to be cool. Ellie Newberger, director of the Family Development Study at Children's Hospital in Boston, believes that the bombardment of children with violence and sexual messages only tends to confuse them (*Newsweek*,

December 1985). This confusion is especially true for youngsters already using drugs and alcohol on a more or less regular basis. Heavy metal is more than music; it is a religion for those young people who feel alienated, resentful, and not part of the majority culture (Gulfport *Sun Herald*, August 1986; Raleigh *Times*, September 1986).

## Religion of Heavy Metal

That word "religion" is not used lightly. For a troubled youngster who views the world through dark glasses, heavy metal is a theology of chaos, violence, and rebellion expressed in thundering rhythm. "Satan is an outcast. I'd rather be an outcast than conform to the majority," says one heavy metal musician (*USA Today*, August 1986). The music is attractive because the drums and the electric guitars, intensified by earphones or powerful amplifiers, focus the limbic (pleasure and emotion) part of the brain on the song. All music appeals in some fashion to the "fun" side of the human mind – that's why humans like it. But research shows that music stimulates, especially accompanied by multisensory input (Steussy, 1985). The sensations are amplified when the youngster is using drugs, particularly marijuana or LSD.

The bass and drums beat of heavy metal is rather like the board a farmer uses to wallop a mule's head – "just to get his attention," as the joke goes. The real problem is the messages of hate, despair, Satan worhip, suicide, deviant sex, and criminal behavior contained in the lyrics and acted out on the stage.

Most parents don't know the words contained in heavy metal rock songs. Most parents don't believe their children know, either. That's a faulty – and potentially dangerous – assumption. Over 50 percent of youngsters in one drug treatment program can write the lyrics to many, many heavy metal songs (King, 1985). For those who can't understand the words in the songs, the lyrics often are printed on the album jackets. For those too illiterate to read the words, the rock stars who stare out from menacing album covers sport pentagrams, studded bracelets, tattoos with the number "666" (the number associated with Satan), suggestive sexual postures, human skulls, or other evidence of recent violence.

Three basic themes underline heavy metal music: violence, sexual deviation, and occult symbolism. These themes are carried out in lyrics, music, and presentation, which includes the album jacket, concert performance, media interviews, stories on the lifestyles of the stars, or rock videos. The raucous, irreverent, aggressive, destructive nature of the lyrics, music, and presentation convinces troubled youngsters that they have tapped a power source (King, 1986).

## Heavy Metal Evolution

By any music lover's yardstick, the Monterey International Pop Festival in June 1967 was one of the finest achievements in rock music. The great ones played there: Janis Joplin, The Who, Jimi Hendrix, The Mamas and the Papas, the Grateful Dead, The Byrds, Jefferson Airplane, Canned Heat, Country Joe and the Fish, and the list goes on. As children of the 1960s, most parents today can remember the names, snap their fingers to the beat, and recapture the mood of that festival and the great Woodstock experience that followed. Out of these festivals came a message from the rock musicians, and from their accompanying media glamorization, that drugs were acceptable. The songs said they were, and many of the best musicians lived and died in the drug culture. Rod "Pigpen" McKernan (Grateful Dead), Keith Moon (The Who), Brian Jones (Rolling Stones), Janis Joplin, and Jimi Hendrix all died from alcohol or other drugs. Books and magazines looking at the history of rock 'n' roll give a great deal of space to the use of marijuana, LSD, and other drugs by the rock stars (Goldberg, June 1987; Herman, 1982).

There was another agenda at those early festivals: Stop the Vietnam War; let black and white love one another; wholesome relationships are always in style. Parents who were teenagers in those days will be hard-pressed to recall songs that urged them to kill, murder, maim, destroy for pleasure, or hurt each other. The greatest single message was love.

The legacy of 1960s rock music was the tendency to adopt simple solutions for very complex problems: Love is the answer. Music transcended the day-to-day routine of life. Rock musicians led an existence on a level that made them gods and goddesses to the fans.

The magic ingredient and simplest solution to complex problems was drug use. Those early musicians used drugs. Newspapers followed their exploits. Young fans of the 1960s were using drugs and became likewise transported in the same world of the musician's music.

Most youngsters in that era survived. The power in that music was its demand for change, for rebellion against the injustices adult society was perpetrating. The music said: Stop the war, eliminate segregation, and end repressive views of sex. What remains in the 1980s is the predisposition to drugs. The causes for which the music and the beat clamored are gone. In the 1980s vacuum of aimless rebellion and personal impotency, heavy metal music remains.

Heavy metal music got its beginnings in England in poverty-stricken areas. The bands played in nightclubs, called death clubs, and achieved a lot of success among the angry and alienated young people. Chief among these bands was Black Sabbath and its lead singer, Ozzy Osbourne. Black Sabbath had been successful since the late 1960s. But Osbourne, now on his own, became a god to a large number of young people.

Even when the media coverage and "mainstream" American attention to a heavy metal group subsided, the popularity of these musicians continued among young people in trouble with drugs. Encapsulated in earphones or sandwiched between powerful amps, these youngsters hear in the music something most adults and other teenagers don't understand.

## Lakeside Study

A retrospective study of 242 male and 228 female adolescent patients examined music preference, delinquency pattern, and drug use. The patients were divided into three categories:

1. Patients who were treated primarily for drug and alcohol problems as well as the emotional and family problems coming from their drug use. These patients were chemically dependent (CDC).

2. Patients with the primary problem of a psychiatric and/or conduct disorder, but who also had a history of drug abuse (though not as extensive as those in category 1).

3. Patients with psychiatric and/or conduct disorder who did

not have a history of drug abuse.

The patients came from Memphis, and Shelby County, Tennessee, and a surrounding 100-mile radius that included smaller cities and rural areas in Tennessee, Arkansas, and Mississippi. The patients predominantly were white, from various socioeconomic backgrounds, and ranged in age from 13 through 17 (a few patients were 18).

The study divided the music into eight categories: heavy metal, acid rock, hard core, pop, hard rock/rap, country, Hank Williams Jr., and unspecified. The names of 50 groups in the different categories were listed. Hank Williams Jr. seemed to have a broader appeal than other country performers, so he was listed separately. "Unspecified responses" refers to those who listen primarily to the radio. The placement of a group in a particular category was subjective, and certainly there may be some disagreement as to the appropriate category. In addition, the study determined the patients' participation in three categories of delinquent behavior – stealing, drug dealing, and violence. Violence was described as documented episodes of physical aggression at home or outside, and/or more than an isolated episode of property destruction. An additional category looked at involvement in sexual activity.

The following are the results of the study: Out of 203 patients admitted primarily because of chemical dependence (133 males and 70 females), 57.1 percent preferred heavy metal as their first choice in type of music. It is interesting to note that only 2 percent listed heavy metal as a second choice in music preference. Chemically dependent youngsters had a 74.4 percent incidence of violence, while 49.8 percent of them stole. Sexual activity was 71.9 percent.

Out of 145 patients admitted with behavior problems and some drugs (57 males and 88 females), 39.3 percent gave heavy metal as the first choice, with pop music chosen by 27.6 percent. No patients listed heavy metal as a second choice. Delinquent behavior of violence appeared in 57.9 percent and stealing among 27.6 percent. Also high was sexual activity, at 52.4 percent.

Of the 122 patients who did not use drugs (52 males and 70 females), only 16.4 percent gave heavy metal as a first music preference and 0.8 percent as a second preference. The percentages preferring popular music rose to 42.6 percent and 9.8 percent for first and second choices, respectively, for a total of 52.5 percent. It is interesting to note that only 39.3 percent of these patients had a history of violence, and 14.8 percent were into stealing. The incidence of sexual activity also was lower, at 24.6 percent (King, 1988).

What conclusions can be draw from these data? First, disturbed youngsters and youths who use drugs exhibit a high incidence of violent behavior and sexual activity. This would go together with the brain's lack of ability to adequately control the sexual and aggressive drives as a result of developmental shortcomings, psychiatric problems, and drugs. The use of drugs by disturbed teenagers also is alarmingly high at 74 percent of admissions, or 348 out of 470 patients. These statistics agree with the studies done by Dr. Marc Gold and Dr. Herb Roehrick of Fair Oaks Hospital in New Jersey, showing a high degree of drug abuse in adolescent psychiatric patients (Gold, 1986-87).

The music preference study pointed to a high number of disturbed adolescents who listen to "disturbing" music. The themes of violence, hate, rebellion, primitive sex, and, as the teens call it, "head banging" music has appeal for both drug-using and non-drug-using disturbed adolescents. This appeal, however, is increased markedly when the adolescent uses drugs as a part of his lifestyle, and it is quite a significant part of the day-to-day activity and life of a majority of chemically dependent adolescents. The chemically dependent adolescent appears to have a lifestyle of violence, stealing, high sexual activity, and heavy metal. Likewise, adolescents with only some drug use also exhibit a high degree of violence and sexual activity, though less stealing. This may be related to sporadic or infrequent drug use. Heavy metal still was a significant part of the lifestyle for these youngsters, but pop did come a closer second. Those teenagers who were psychiatrically impaired but not involved with drugs had the lowest rates of stealing, violence, sexual activity, and heavy metal listening.

The chemically dependent youngsters in treatment say they listen to messages that "tell it like it is." "You want to know something about us? You better know our music," said one newly admitted adolescent addict. The message of heavy metal music is that there is a higher power in control of the world, and that power is violence – often violence presided over by Satan. This is something hopeless youngsters can sink their teeth into.

Children who do not identify with the values with which they were raised must identify with something. All youngsters, whether they say so or not, believe in a Higher Power. Troubled youngsters believe the highest power is evil. Heavy metal affirms this theology and puts it to music.

## The Image of Heavy Metal

Bill got into drugs at the invitation of his older brother. But once he had a taste of it, he continued his alcohol and drug-related behavior on his own. After one arrest for public drunkenness, his parents were alerted to trouble. They admitted him to treatment the day he turned up stoned at a mall. He was 16. "I listened to heavy metal music a lot, like AC-DC and KISS. I got into the words and listened to all the negative messages of hate and depression, defiance of authority," Bill said toward the end of his hospitalization. "I began to identify with the image projected by the rock stars. I was filled with hate. Getting stoned and cranking up some heavy metal made me feel okay about me and not see that something was terribly wrong. I wore pentagrams, stole from my family, and became a drug addict. Satan, drugs, and heavy metal were my life."

The link between heavy metal music and violent behavior is being made in an increasing number of murders and suicides. Here are a few of the more sensational examples reported over the past three years in national magazines and daily newspapers:

● The medical examiner investigating the suicide of an 18-year-old cadet at St. John's Military Academy found a human skull and burning candle next to the body. Music from "The Wall" by Pink Floyd, which contained such songs as "Goodbye, Cruel World" and "Waiting for the Worms," played nearby, and the examiner felt that type of music contributed to the suicidal depression (*News Sun*, February 1986).

● The father of a 19-year-old suicide victim in Los Angeles sued singer Ozzy Osbourne unsuccessfully for contributing to the death of his son. The boy was found wearing earphones and apparently had been listening to such Osbourne songs as "Suicide Solution" (Bio-Acoustics Res. Rev., Fall 1986).

• Four teenagers in Bergenfield, New Jersey, commit suicide, all within a short period. Their bond was ". . . music, mainly heavy metal . . . drugs and alcohol also play a part, some of the burnouts said" (*Commercial Appeal*, March 1987).

• A member of the group "Slayer" says his group should not be blamed for a Lake City, Arkansas, man's alleged attack on his parents. Eddie Crigler, 24, is accused of using a knife and a two-by-four studded with nails to beat his parents as they lay in their beds. Crigler reportedly had played a recording of Slayer's "Reign in Blood" for hours on end (*Commercial Appeal*, May 1987).

• The parents of actor Patrick Duffy allegedly were killed by a young man obsessed with the album "Kill 'Em All" by the band Metallica (*People Weekly*, Sept. 26, 1986).

All this is not to say that everyone who listens to heavy metal becomes a deranged killer or commits suicide. But in heavy metal, evil acts are glorified to new heights – particularly in concerts. Gunpowder is lit, humanlike figures are hanged and placed in coffins, demonic figures are produced, and property is destroyed. That is not to mention the language many parents consider objectionable, or the sexual expressions that abound. By the time a heavy metal concert is over, the crowd is whipped into a frenzy. That crowd primarily is youngsters 12 to 18 years old. The on-stage glamorizing of violence and hate is confusing to these young people, who are trying to decide who they should be and what kind of behavior is appropriate for them.

## Parental Responses

After the 1985 Senate subcommittee hearings on rock music, there was a clamor to have government action on lyrics and music. The music industry began using labels which warned parents that some lyrics may be considered objectionable.

The labeling was helpful in this respect – many parents didn't know what the rock music said. The real power in regulating music rests with informed parents. The authority on what is considered objectionable for children should not be determined by a government but by that child's parents. That's where the power to regulate music should be. Regulation does not belong in Congress, in the pulpit, in the newspapers, or with teenagers. Parents should really call the tunes.

The Parents' Music Resource Center (PMRC) in Arlington, Virginia, a group formed out of concern for the type of music attacked during the 1985 Senate hearings, publishes "Let's Talk Rock," a booklet that contains three common-sense suggestions for parents to use in working with teenagers on what music they can hear.

1. Understand and listen to your child's music. Just because you as an adult hate the sound, don't throw it out. Remember what your mother said about the Beatles or Elvis? Listen to what your children are playing and singing; ask them if the words to those songs agree with what the family believes. Keep the discussion of the music focused on content, not the style of the song. A dictatorial approach can drive a normal teenager to take seriously the antiestablishment values in the songs.

2. Establish guidlines about the types of music that won't be allowed and be prepared to follow up with disciplinary action. Let your child know that songs glorifying the occult, violence, and oppressive sex won't be entertained in your home. Be specific and explain. Permit discussion; compromise when you feel you can. Then make a ruling and prepare to live by it.

3. Enforce the established guidelines. One aspect of your program should be that, if your child buys an album with an objectionable song on it, you will either buy the record from him or return it to the store. That way he isn't penalized for being honest or going along with the program (PMRC, 1986).

For a youngster already in serious trouble, the best solution is the most drastic. In good hospital treatment programs, a patient must surrender all his rock music, his videos, tee shirts, and heavy metal gear as soon as he is admitted. He may not have them for a year so that he is not influenced again by musical feelings of resentment, hate, and the urge to party – an expression that means to use drugs, perform sex, and listen to music. In fact, in some treatments the patient is required to destroy these things before he is considered well enough to go home.

Such is the power of music.

## COMPARISON OF ADOLESCENT PATIENTS
## ADMITTED FOR DRUG AND PSYCHIATRIC PROBLEMS

| Unit | N | Heavy Metal (%) | Violence (%) | Stealing (%) | Sexual Activity (%) |
|---|---|---|---|---|---|
| Chemically Dependent Component | 203 | 59.1 | 74.4 | 49.8 | 71.9 |
| Gen. Psych. Who Use Drugs | 145 | 39.3 | 57.9 | 27.6 | 52.4 |
| Gen. Psych. Who Don't Use Drugs | 122 | 17.2 | 39.3 | 14.8 | 24.6 |
| TOTAL | 470 | 42.1 | 60.2 | 33.8 | 53.6 |

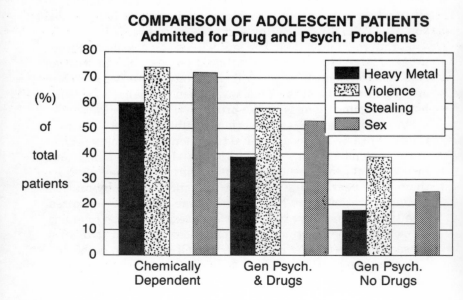

**COMPARISON OF ADOLESCENT PATIENTS**
**Admitted for Drug and Psych. Problems**

# Chapter Seven

Bettleheim, B. "TV Stereotypes Devastating to Young Minds," *US News and World Report*, 55, October 1985.

Bio-Acoustics Research Review. "IBAR Asked to Study Ozzy Osbourne Music," Vol. 1, No. 1, Fall 1986.

Branston, John. "Metal Malady," *Commercial Appeal* Magazine, Memphis, Tennessee, Jan. 5, 1986.

Breskin, D. "Kids in the Dark," *Rolling Stone* Magazine, Straight Arrow Publishers, Nov. 22, 1984.

*Commercial Appeal* (Memphis). "Rock Cited for Bad Vibrations," Ann Landers column, July 27, 1985; "Singer Disputes Music Linked to Man's Attack," Associated Press, May 30, 1987; "Tough Front of Burnouts Pierced by Teen Suicides," *New York Times*, March 14, 1987.

Donovan, J. E.; Jessor, R. "Structure of Problem Behavior in Adolesence and Young Adulthood," J. Counsel Clin. Psychol. 53:89-904, 1985.

Ft. Myers *News Press*. "Psychiatrist Says Teens Tune in to Trouble with Heavy Metal Music," May 20, 1986.

Gold, M.; Roehrick, H. "Diagnosis of Substance Abuse in an Adolescent Population," Int. J. Psych. in Med., Vol. 16, No. 2, 137-142, 1986-87.

Goldberg, M. "Monterey Pop. The Dawning of An Age," *Rolling Stone* Magazine, Straight Arrow Publishers, June 4, 1987.

Gore, T. Raising PG Kids in an X-Rated Society, Abington Press, Nashville, 1987.

Gulfport *Sun Herald*. "Psychiatrist Blasts Drugs, Heavy Metal," Aug. 13, 1986.

Herman, G. "Rock-n-Roll Babylon," Courage Books, Philadelphia, 1982.

Hunter, R. "The Storming of the Mind," NY Anchor Books, 1972.

King, P. "Heavy Metal: A New Religion," hearing before Committee on Commerce, 99th Congress, U.S. Printing Office, Washington, D.C., 1985.

King, P. Sex, Drugs, Rock-n-Roll, Southeast Conference on Alcohol and Drugs (SECAD)-West, Salt Lake City, April 2, 1987.

King, P. Adolescent Addiction: From Satan to Spirituality, Southeast Conference on Alcohol and Drugs, Atlanta, Dec. 4, 1986.

King, P. Teenage Drug Culture, American Medical Society on Alcoholism and Other Drug Dependencies convention, Cleveland, April 25, 1987.

King, P. "The Relationship Between Drug Use and Heavy Metal Music in Adolescents," Postgraduate Medicine Vol. 83, No. 5, McGraw Hill Publishing Company, Minneapolis, April 1988.

*News Sun* (Waukegan, Illinois), "Rock Music Blamed in Teen Death," United Press International, Feb. 13, 1986.

*Newsweek*, "MTV's Message," Dec. 30, 1985.

Parents Music Resource Center. "Let's Talk Rock – A Primer for Parents," published by the Parents Music Resource Center, 1986.

*People Weekly*, "A World Away From Dallas, Patrick Duffy's Parents Are Slain in Their Montana Tavern," written by Ron Labrecque, Time and Life Building, New York, Sept. 26, 1986.

*Raleigh Times*, "National Authority Links Teenagers Drug Abuse to Sexy, Sordid Music," Sept. 16, 1986.

Stantberg, M. "Sounds of Silence Deadly?" *The Register-Guard*, Eugene, Oregon, Nov. 29, 1986.

Steussey, J. "Statements at Senate Subcommittee Hearings," hearing before Committee on Commerce, 99th Congress, U.S. Printing Office, Washington, D.C., 1985.

*USA Today*, "Heavy Metal Bands Rock Generations," Life Section, Aug. 18, 1986.

*US Journal of Drug and Alcohol Dependence*, "Lighten Up on Heavy Metal," Vol. 18, No. 4, April 1986.

*US News and World Report*, "Do You Know What Your Children Are Listening To?" Oct. 28, 1985.

*A pentagram inside an art notebook reveals this young patient's involvement with satanism and the violence it spawns.*

## CHAPTER EIGHT

# Nature of the Problem: Violence and Satan

DR. AND MRS. TIM T. WERE TERRIFIED AND BEWILDERED WHEN they discovered 16-year-old Don stealing wooden crosses from graveyards, drawing devils, writing poetry about beasts and blood. Mrs. T., a legal secretary, first became alarmed several months earlier, when Don cut satanic symbols into his arm. Since then he'd become increasingly aggressive, belligerent, and hostile.

George, 14, wrote an essay about Druidism that his high school English teacher thought was pretty good, though a little weird. But then, she observed after he was hospitalized for drug abuse, George was a little strange himself. He wore satanic symbols on his tee shirts and a five-pointed star called a pentagram around his neck, and he was frequently seen in the halls with books about Satan worship.

Blond, blue-eyed Jimmy, 16, sang in the choir at his fundamentalist church. Under his suit and tie he wore a rock tee shirt with satanic symbols on it. He later told his counselor that this kept the minister away . . . and Satan closer to his heart.

All these youngsters were white and came from middle-to-upper-class families (black teenagers do not appear to identify with the satanic phenomenon). These youngsters had loving, caring, intelligent, concerned parents who were unaware of their children's problems until they became acute. Until they began getting into trouble, the teenagers made average grades in school. Two attended church regularly, one had no religious affiliation, and the fourth was an occasional churchgoer.

In short, these were not extraordinary youngsters who suffered in a traumatic home situation. They were just normal suburban teenagers like the ones who hang out at the drive-in or the mall on Saturdays.

Teenagers who are looking to the occult as the power in their lives have good reason to choose that route. They certainly don't believe God has any place in their sick existence. Their behavior is so far out of control that they have to check out unorthodox places for a force to rule their chaotic world. Traditional power sources have fizzled and shorted out for these youngsters.

Although they would rather die than admit it, these troubled teenagers no longer are in control of themselves. Outside influences have imprisoned them. Long-term use of drugs and alcohol have created a chemical imbalance that lasts far beyond the effective time of the average illegal drug. This imbalance has opened their minds to ideas that wouldn't be considered under normal circumstances. As one 17-year-old said, "I'd have never gotten interested in Pink Floyd's 'The Wall' if I didn't smoke marijuana."

In many cases, the drugs generate a type of paranoia that stays with children after drug use ceases. Therefore, it is most likely that troubled teenagers will see only evil, confusion, chaos, condemnation, and abuse in their world. And who in American culture is in charge of such a world? Satan.

Youngsters who are starting to believe the devil is in charge of the universe generally make up their theology as a by-product of their addiction. Only rarely are they attached to some formal or adult satanic organization. What they believe about Satan and the power of evil, they garner through hours of listening to heavy metal music, years of imagining the devil as preached from the pulpit, reading volumes on the occult such as "Necronomicon" (1980), and months of living in their own hell of chemicals.

Teenagers begin by dabbling in the occult and flaunting satanic symbols. Their brains are so changed by alcohol and other drugs that professional intervention is the only solution. They have completed their slide into hell and represent a genuine threat to public safety.

## Nature of the Belief

Of 203 teenagers admitted to Charter Lakeside Hospital in a three-year period for drug or alcohol abuse, over half owned Black Rock tee shirts, posters, tapes, or albums with such satanic or demonic symbols as pentagrams, upside-down crosses, and monstrous caricatures. Between 15 and 20 of these teenagers admitted to participating in some kind of devil worship – either in group ceremonies or by lighting candles, burning incense, studying satanic literature, or praying to Satan. These 15 or 20 teenagers all began with satanic symbols, reciting rock lyrics praising Satan, and cited rock musicians with the most demonic images as their heroes.

Thanks to the national publicity surrounding some youthful murderers, suicide victims, and sensational killers, child psychologists and psychiatrists are waking up to the problem of self-styled satanism. The horror is not in the numbers of teenagers engaged in the practice; the frightening thing is what youngsters are capable of when they get into the most modest form of satanic worship. From a youngster's point of view, the pull of satanism is understandable. Once a teenager is into the drug- and alcohol-dependent lifestyle – which glorifies chaos and disorder, violence, hate, lying, manipulating, stealing, and vandalism – some other need is triggered. He craves some kind of higher power to validate all the madness.

Satanism is a youngster's attempt to bring order and authority into his life. It is an attempt to establish boundaries, even if the "boundaries" are considered depraved by most of society. Since his values and morals tell him his behavior is unacceptable, he searches not for a way to make what he has done appear right, as an adult would, but for some source authority to approve his behavior.

Self-styled satanism seems to be the answer when a teenager's traditional value system cries out in alarm. The disturbed teenager sees satanism, which preaches violence and antisocial behavior, as the philosophy or value system to fit the way he is feeling and to replace those nagging old values echoing in the back of his head.

Once he's adopted self-styled satanism, the teenager is as dangerous as a loaded gun in a kindergarten. The alcohol and other drugs have interrupted the child's rational thinking processes and robbed him of impulse control, while the music he chooses has put him in the mood for raising hell (literally), evil, suicide, murder, or giving/receiving sexual abuse. A belief in Satan gives him the authority for doing things he could never before bring himself to do – even when he was stoned or drunk.

Satan, it should be pointed out, never has been associated with the women's liberation movement. The highest form of satanic sacrifice is a woman dressed in white, trussed up like a turkey, and placed on a black altar. Very few teenage females get involved in satanic rituals or beliefs unless forced to do so by their boyfriends. Generally speaking, satanism is a macho male philosophy.

## Drugs, Music, Devils, and Murder

In looking at some of the more sensational murder cases in the news, several common elements emerge: the satanic interest of the accused murderers, their heavy drug use, and their obsession with heavy metal music.

The best known of these murder cases is the 1969 Tate-LaBianca murders by members of the Manson family who regularly took psychedelic drugs and studied Revelations in the Bible as the battle plan for the new order (Bugliosi, 1975). Probably the next most publicized murderer is David "Son of Sam" Berkowitz, who liked to take psychedelic drugs and discuss the apocalyptic significance of a rock album by Black Sabbath (Conway, 1979). He is in prison for murdering seven persons. New York police have investigated reports linking Berkowitz to a satanic cult in that city.

Middle Amercia was rocked in 1985 by the arrest of Ricky Kasso in Northport, New York, for torturing another teenager, stabbing out his eyes, forcing him to cry how he loved Satan, and then finishing him off while heavy metal music blared. The violence started over a drug deal. Later, in jail, Kasso hanged himself (Breskin, 1984).

The most recent case was the arrest of accused "Night Stalker" Richard Ramirez, charged with killing 14 people. The Night

Stalker apparently spray-painted pentagrams on the walls of the homes he ransacked. Ramirez had a pentagram tattooed on his hand and was obsessed with the heavy metal music group AC-DC (Flood, September 1985).

Since 1985, the incidence of satanic rituals being involved in murder or animal mutilation or suicide has been on the up- swing, if cases reported in the public press count for anything. As reported in newspapers and magazines, drugs, music, and the devil also were involved in such less-publicized murder cases as the following:

• Shawn Sellers, 17, convicted murderer and youngest of 66 inmates on the Oklahoma State Penitentiary death row. His defense argued that his obsession with Satan constituted insanity (*People Weekly*, Dec. 1, 1986).

• A 14-year-old Catholic high school teenager in New Jersey obsessed with the occult and heavy metal music. He killed his mother and attempted to kill his father and brother. Afterwards, he slit his wrists and throat (*Commercial Appeal*, Jan. 13, 1988).

• The body of a 19-year-old Joplin, Missouri, boy found in a well together with the remains of two squirrels and a recently killed cat (*Commercial Appeal*, 1987).

• Five youthful devil worshipers in Houston, accused of beat- ing, choking, and stabbing to death a young man behind a cemetery, just to see someone die (Meckel, September 1985).

• A 15-year-old boy accused of murdering his 16-year-old girlfriend, then flying to San Antonio to admit himself to a drug rehabilitation program. The girlfriend once had told a friend the young man was a devil worshiper – something the boy's mother later confirmed (Douglas, September 1985).

These cases do not suggest that every self-styled satanist is a murderer, or even that every boy wearing a black tee shirt and a cross in the left ear is a satanist. They do demonstrate the potential for bizarre and sick behavior when a child with chemi- cally altered thought processes begins to believe he has a higher authority giving him permission to act in an antisocial way. Widespread fascination with the occult is part of the teenage drug culture. The violence comes from the chemical action on the teenage brain, encouraged by heavy metal music. Satan validates the act once it is committed. Youngsters are comfortable working under such a higher authority, and they are extremely loyal.

Sixteen-year-old Bob, tall, thin, and dark-haired, said he'd always been fascinated with evil, monsters, and creature feature movies as a child. As a teenager he enjoyed the music and antics of the heavy metal group KISS. "They appeared real evil and demonic," he said.

Later, as Bob became more interested in drugs, he started wearing eyeliner, leather jackets, and spikes to look like the KISS musicians. "I really enjoyed scaring people and being called evil and crazy," he recalled. One day, he and his friend Tom, another drug-dependent teenager, met a man who attended a satanic worship service. Bob discovered Tom knew something about Satan, too. Bob decided to attend the local church of Satan. Later, Bob would convince Tom to join him at the satanic service.

"The first time I went was the only time I saw any violence there," Bob said. "They cut this guy's wrist and filled a cup of blood for me to drink. I was learning chants and a prayer. I requested things from Satan during rituals. I got a "high" out of it. The more I went the more powerful I felt. I never saw or participated in any sacrifices, but I wanted to. I thought that would be the ultimate "high."

Shortly after he began attending the Satanic Church, someone burned the building down. Bob's fellow worshipers were furious. "I know they killed someone they thought had something to do with burning the church down. My friend tried to get me, but I wasn't home. I had a lot of anger about the church, and I would have gone and killed him without any thought about it." Bob was brought into treatment when his parents became worried that he'd commit suicide.

## Rebellion or Religion

In the past, mental health care officials considered satanic symbols part of the teenager's rebellion, and the concert or black tee shirts adorned with pentagrams and the number "666" as the regulation uniform of that rebellion. Nobody bothered to probe deeper.

What adolescent counselors are slowly learning about satanic symbols is that these are early signs of belief and not mere trappings of youthful rebellion. Left unchecked, these symbols are followed by others until the youngster is very heavily into satanism. Ask a youngster why he is wearing black or a studded bracelet, and he'll give a very scary response: He wants to look "bad" and "evil." As Bob's story shows, the teenager is attracted to satanism because it makes him feel powerful (Flood, 1985).

Youngsters even go to local bookstores to buy — and study — tomes on druidism, satan worship, Egyptian magic, and ancient Hebrew mysticism. Remember, these messed-up youngsters are the same ones who cannot fathom the mysteries of geometry or American history. These signs of self-styled satanism actually are the last red flags a teenager throws up before he does serious harm to himself or others. In the final stages, it is not just another sign of youthful rebellion like a Mohawk haircut or a black leather jacket.

A music teacher in a New Jersey public high school was not surprised to hear satanism was on the rise among troubled American teenagers. She said she saw it all the time in the corridors of her school, where wealthy families sent their teen-agers: black leather jackets with the devil painted on the back, tattoos on forearms, notebooks with "666" and "Lord Satan" scrawled on them, upside-down crosses pierced into the left earlobes of boys. "You have to wonder, though," she said, "how much of this is thumbing their noses at adults, and how much do they really believe?"

Two of the crucial elements in distinguishing rebellion or a passing interest with heavy metal music from the beginnings of genuine satanic belief are time and behavior. Parents should ask themselves: Did the satanic symbols appear from out of the blue, or have they been popping up sporadically and secretly over the weeks? Symbols that seem to pop out overnight usually are like teenage acne — pretty normal — and are gone just as quickly as any other blemish when parents apply the proper soap and water. Satanic symbols that multiply over time and are something parents accidentally stumble over can mean trouble. Parents should sit down and decide whether this destructive, out-of-control behavior and bizarre appearance has been growing stronger over time, or whether this smart-aleck apparition who calls you Mom and Dad is a new phenomenon. A fleeting interest in the occult is one thing; obsession with it is quite another.

Once a teenager is admitted to treatment, there is no doubt. A child hospitalized with the five-pointed star of the devil tattooed on his arm or the number of the beast ("666") written on his personal articles is at the very least in the first stage of self-styled satanism. Parents should understand that rebellions can be quashed; belief cannot without professional help.

Chaplain Alan Bell of Charter Lakeside Hospital in Memphis said that one of the scariest things about self-styled satanists is the strength of their belief. With most cults or fanatical religious groups, even the strongest converts waiver and fall away after time. Such is not the case with teenagers who have adopted satanism. "I don't see kids running away from Satan. They become hypnotized," Bell says.

The symbolism in the downward slide of a troubled teenager is irresistible. An attitude of anger and resentment is a youngster's first overt sign that trouble is brewing, and at the bottom of his pit of hopelessness, despair, and destruction is the fiery image of a masterful Satan. By the time a youngster begins drawing pentagrams and praying to Satan for order in his world of madness, he is so deeply into mind-altering drugs that he is dangerous to himself and others.

Teenagers in trouble are not like comedian Flip Wilson. When they say "the devil made me do it," they aren't joking.

### Chapter Eight

Breskin, D. "Kids in the Dark," written for *Rolling Stone* Magazine, Nov. 22, 1984.

Bugliosi, V. Helter Skelter: The True Story of the Manson Murders, Bantam, New York, 1975.

*Commercial Appeal*, Memphis, "Cult links are sought in slaying," Dec. 11, 1987.

*Commercial Appeal*, Memphis, "Devil pushed teen over the brink, police say," Associated Press, Newark, New Jersey, Jan. 13, 1988.

Conway, F., and Siegelman, J. Snapping, Delta Books, New York, 1979.

Douglas, J. "Slaying suspect, 15, held at drug center," Houston *Post*, Sept. 11, 1985.

Flood, M. "Devil worship: what's behind it?" Houston *Post*, Sept. 15, 1985.

Mickel, R. "Judge cuts bail for suspected devil worshippers," Houston *Post*, Sept. 12, 1985.

Necronomicon, edited with an introduction by Simon, Avon Books, New York, 1980.

*People Weekly*, "A Boy's Love of Satan Ends in Murder, a Death Sentence – and Grisly Memories," written by Michelle Green, reported by Civia Tamarkin, Time and Life Building, New York, Dec. 1, 1986.

*A 17-year-old's description of treatment shows the necessity of removing media influence before the principles of a Twelve Step program could be meaningful.*

# CHAPTER NINE

# The Power
# of the Twelve Steps

FOR MILLIONS OF CHEMICALLY DEPENDENT CHILDREN AND adults, there are 12 steps on the road back from drugs, promiscuous sex, and violence. These are the Twelve Steps developed by Alcoholics Anonymous, the most successful method of recovering from drug or alcohol addiction. While it works, the Twelve Step program seems paradoxical: To gain control, the addict must give up control. Put another way, to gain control of his life, the addict must give up the obsession to control his use of alcohol or other drugs. Central to this approach is a new belief system that focuses on a Higher Power and the needs of others rather than on the satisfaction of one's selfish goals and the pursuit of personal power.

Although it began as a program for adults, AA is a powerful tool for chemically addicted youngsters as well. The secret lies in the spiritual nature of the concept. AA acts to change the youngster's internal belief system. This spiritual approach to a lifetime solution of a physical problem has proven effective for chemically dependent people for more than 50 years.

In 1944, the American Medical Association recognized that alcoholism is a disease and applauded the role of Alcoholics Anonymous in helping alcoholics (Jellineck, E.M., 1960; Steinberg, 1987). AA is so tremendously popular because it has a spiritual element that makes long-term successful recovery possible (Miller, 1987). The goal of inpatient treatment, certainly for adults, is to accept a life of recovery through the principles of AA. Many adult treatment programs motivate their patients to become involved in AA. In fact, the numbers of alcoholics who saw treatment as the motivating force for entry into AA increased from 26 percent to 36 percent from 1980 to 1986 (*Alcoholism and Addiction*, 1987). Later came the increased recognition of other chemical dependencies as diseases (Gold, 1984), and the growth of Narcotics Anonymous (NA) and more recently, Cocaine Anonymous (CA). These self-help programs as well as others – including Al-Anon, Overeaters Anonymous, and Emotions Anonymous – all use the principles of the original Twelve Steps of AA as their program foundation.

AA began with the efforts of two alcoholics who remained in recovery through working with other alcoholics. Bill Wilson had failed numerous times to achieve sobriety (Carl Jung was said to have told an alcoholic patient that therapy would not work, but that possibly, a spiritual experience might lead to a conversion and recovery). An old acquaintance who became sober through a spiritual group could not help Bill directly but planted the seed for the need of a spiritual experience. In December 1934, while under the care of Dr. William Silkworth, Bill had a spiritual experience and never returned to alcohol. Later, he realized that the only way to remain sober was to work with other alcoholics. In Akron, Ohio, in 1935, Bill was on the verge of relapse again when he met another alcoholic, Dr. Robert Smith. Together they started AA.

The basic unit of AA is the "group," in which alcoholics gather to share of themselves so they may recover from alcoholism. The alcoholics learn that a Higher Power works through the group to achieve in each member a sense of spiritual growth (Clinebell, 1979). The key element is the surrender of one's willfulness to the will of a Higher Power. The individual must give up a part of his individuality to the group, take risks in the group, and be honest, open, and willing. By learning to care more for others and less about him/herself, the craving for alcohol diminishes.

However, the urge to drink comes back unless he or she continues to go to meetings to recharge the spiritual experience. God is perceived as working through the group, and therefore the individual must surrender his will to the group (Stuckey, 1985). Continuing to go to AA does recharge the spiritual experience, but it also prevents something called denial from creeping back in each time a person identifies him/herself as an alcoholic. It also aids in the long-term goal of swapping a negative identity as a "drunk" or addict for a positive identity as a recovering alcoholic or addict. For the self-centered chemically dependent person, there is something uniquely healing about being willing to ask for help from others. That is what a person is doing by turning up at an AA meeting.

The Twelve Steps represent the work in attitude change necessary to achieve sobriety. Working the Steps is the spiritual growth. The Steps refer to God (Steps two, three, five, six, seven, and eleven), others (Steps five, eight, nine, and twelve), and self (Steps one, four, five, and ten). The goal is the ability to live in harmony with God, self, and others. This is seen as a spiritual need to be fulfilled in order to grow (Reiners, 1980).

## Admitting Powerlessness: Step One

The work in treatment begins with the First Step, in which denial is exposed and worked through. The group confronts the alcoholic with the consequences of his chemical use, and in this way he comes to realize that his life has been unmanageable. The onset and progression of the disease of chemical dependency is not seen by the addict, so for him or her it does not exist. Certain defense patterns are used to keep the addict's denial strong. These include rationalization, projection, and repression.

Rationalization explains away behaviors caused by drugs by focusing on some explanation other than the chemicals.

Projection is the placement of hate, especially self-hate, onto others and therefore avoiding one's own negative feelings.

Repression is the ability to block out that which is painful and unpleasant (Hamel, 1985). This last defense to deny the problem is especially effective for young people who do not look at the effects of their behavior on such loved ones as parents. The youngster's denial is shared by enablers – the family, significant others, and even some professionals. The enabler protects the alcoholic from the harmful consequences of his drinking (Johnson Institute, 1982). As a result, he is not adversely affected and therefore has no reason to stop using. A more modern concept is codependency, which identifies the enabler as dependent on the alcoholic and the illness for an identity (Cocores, 1987). The codependent with emotional or adjustment problems may turn to codependent treatment or to Al-Anon for assistance.

The denial system is destroyed when the alcoholic can get up in front of his or her peers and state, "My name is ———, and I'm an alcoholic." The establishment of an identity of being an alcoholic within the peer group is an admittance that one cannot drink; otherwise it's back to compulsive use and relapse.

Step One simply states: "We admitted we were powerless over alcohol (or drugs) – that our lives had become unmanageable." The word powerless means that the use of alcohol or drugs has become more important than any rational reason to stop. Even in the face of family problems, school difficulties, and increasing trouble with the law, a youngster's drug use continues. The child is enslaved by the compulsion to experience again the same drug feeling. There is a loss of the power of choice.

For someone to even begin Step One, he has to be held responsible for his own problem. Often, there is denial on the part of teenagers and parents. Even some treatment professionals see drug use as the parents' problem. But once parents refuse to accept this projection and tell the child that he is sick and in need of treatment, rehabilitation is possible.

In the beginning of treatment, the child will look at the drug use to see how it hurt his functioning and made everyone unhappy. The drugs are seen as "evil." Actually, the problem is not in the alcohol or drug, since millions are able to use alcohol or other chemicals socially without getting into difficulty. The problem is the user's need for the chemical. This may be seen as a compulsive need for a mood-altering experience to either melt away anxiety, deal with frustration, or just have fun. The addiction is in terms of that ever-growing need coupled with the belief that the alcohol or the drug will solve the problem. The child structures his life around opportunities to get "high." Using chemicals then becomes the most important event in the teenager's daily life.

The admission of powerlessness, therefore, requires the drug user to admit he has a need (compulsion) for the chemical that is different from a pattern of social use. He is different, and that difference makes him unable to use mood-altering substances without becoming chemically dependent. In admitting dependence, he must be able to surrender his "pride" and his obsession to take risks (Bateson, 1972). Unfortunately, unless there is a spiritual change, the young person feels he has learned so much about addiction and has done so well in counseling that he should be able to use drugs without again becoming dependent. That is why most drug education fails to stop or cure addiction (Mann, 1987). This failure is acute especially when the dangers are exaggerated to attempt to create fear, as was done with marijuana users, reports Dr. Joel Moskowitz at the University of California at Berkeley. Research shows that "those programs have not worked," states Dr. Gilbert J. Botvin of Cornell Medical College (Kerr, 1986).

Admission of powerlessness entails the admission of an illness that makes the addict or alcoholic different from the rest of the population. The problem lies in the compulsive illness, and not in the family, the school, or in society. To realize this, the chemically dependent person must overcome personal grandiosity and accept personal humility. Too often, young people feel that they are the masters of their homes. No one tells them what to do; they tell others.

In a situation where the child is the power, it obviously is necessary to give up the power in order to admit having defects leading to powerlessness over chemicals. Taking AA's Step One is a crucial step not only in treatment of chemical dependency but in accepting one's character flaws and giving up feeling powerful. Chemically dependent young people who are acting like gods must join the rest of the world of "defective" human beings. Defeat of a narcissistic or self-centered orientation is the goal of primary treatment for adolescents and a necessary prerequisite for taking Step One. Taking Step One automatically puts a troubled youngster in a new peer group. And this peer group is closer to adulthood than he is. Chemically dependent youngsters are helpless to function in society, yet they are rapidly approaching the age where they must begin assuming adult responsibilities. The fantasy of competence is kept alive when childrens' real needs are cared for by adults while the child play-acts with peers at being "mature" through sexual behavior, violence, and the use of drugs.

The insanity in this situation is that it denies the young person the opportunity to develop the emotional skills necessary to handle growing up in a complex society. Instead of facing this helplessness, the young person becomes more angry and resentful. He takes his anger out on parents or other adults who accept this behavior. Much of his hate, rebelliousness, and resentment is reinforced by the peer group. The youngster, a child who cannot stand on his own beliefs, has an inordinate need to fit into a group and to follow the attitudes of others within the group. The members of the peer group, also angry and resentful, reinforce this attitude. The need for group approval and following the group attitude makes for so-called "peer pressure."

Obviously, for treatment to succeed, the peer group must be changed. Involvement in AA or NA for the youth, and Al-Anon or Tough Love for parents, satisfies the need for group support in a positive direction. The group works on coping with one's problems and overcoming feelings of helplessness and resentment. The ultimate result of successful involvement in AA/NA and Al-Anon is the child's willingness to be self-responsible while parents learn to refuse responsibility for another's behavior. Both child and adult acknowledge their need for ongoing support from the groups to accomplish these goals.

This Step One of admitting helplessness cannot be carried through alone. That is the reason for group meetings. The use of the words "we" and "our" in those meetings and in AA literature shows the strength in admitting the powerlessness and affirms that it is okay to make that admission. The chemically dependent young person who has a desire to quit can find a strong alliance with the others in the group who also are fighting the compulsion. The result is the beginning of new relationships with the common goal of dealing with the obsession and compulsion with chemicals. Moving away from the self and toward the group makes this possible. Once that movement is successful, the need to replace drugs with a spiritual recovery becomes real for a child.

## Belief in Some Greater Power: Step Two

The Higher Power referred to in Step Two can be best understood as one whom the adolescent looks up to with respect. In a spiritual recovery, all adults who lead their own lives along spiritual principles can be considered higher powers, but this is not what occurs in the *beginning* of recovery. The young person in AA or NA chooses a sponsor who represents someone further along in the program. The sponsor has been sober long enough to be a higher power but also can still remember what it's like to make the necessary value and life changes for recovery to occur. Decision-making is quite difficult, as the youngster feels stressed both within himself and from peers. Facing each day without escape to drugs is extremely difficult and painful.

A great emphasis needs to be given to reading recovery material. This includes the Big Book, the basic text of Alcoholics Anonymous, and "Twelve Steps and Twelve Traditions." These books provide the spiritual focus necessary to recovery.

Attendance at meetings several times per week and obtaining a sponsor will lead the young person further into the program. Parents at this point must be involved in a parent's support group and Al-Anon if they are to develop the attitude necessary to help themselves and their child.

In a spiritual recovery, the youngster sees that he no longer has to try to control other people and circumstances. The person learns to live a day at a time and, with an attitude of acceptance, finds he is able to deal with life. He learns to take pleasure in the events that go well and not let adversity overwhelm him. An acceptance of God's will and a surrender of self-will are crucial elements in being able to make it.

Much of this is stated quite well in Steps Two and Three of AA.

Step Two: "Came to believe that a Power greater than ourselves could restore us to sanity."

Step Three: "Made a decision to turn our will and our lives over to the care of God *as we understood Him.*"

Explanations of these Steps and all the Steps are found in "Alcoholics Anonymous" (the Big Book) and "Twelve Steps and Twelve Traditions." The sanity referred to in Step Two is to use the power of God to help reverse the self-will, insane relationships, images, and compulsive behavior. In addition, the words "our," "we," and "us" are used to show a common group bonding on a spiritual level. The emphasis continues to be away from self and towards God and the fellowship of AA. It is through this process that one develops a sensitivity to others and builds relationships on a meaningful and spiritual level.

Again, it is important to note the use of the words "we", "us," and "our" in the Twelve Steps. (See Appendix.) Although each chemically dependent person must work out his/her own program, the spiritual power is in the group. This is another example of moving away from the emphasis on oneself and toward placing that power in the group, for guidance, and then to God. The involvement in fellowship, sharing, and love gives the individual that crucial element to deal effectively with the inner compulsion to drink and use drugs. The chemically dependent person requires a structured system to help him achieve this focus once he becomes abstinent.

Prayers almost always are said at AA meetings. At first glance, this gives the appearance of a religious meeting, and therefore the misconception develops that AA is another religion. Deeper involvement, though, shows that spirituality is a far more basic concept and that talking about God isn't necessarily religion. The act of prayer is very important since it requires the person who is hedonistic, self-centered, wantonly using drugs, and abusing relationships to look to guidance from a Higher Power outside himself. In AA he is giving up that self-centered orientation and turning his will over to the care of God. However, prayer is useless if one is praying just for God to serve man. That is a self-centered attitude. It is, therefore, important to use prayers that have been standardized because these prayers take the emphasis away from the individual and again put everything in God's hands.

Clearly, the goal by Step Three is to have a child abandon his self-centeredness, find a Higher Power, and accept life as it is without resentment. Self-centeredness, caring only about the self and what feels good, is seen as a basic problem area for those who are chemically dependent.

"Selfishness — self-centeredness! That, we think, is the root of our troubles . . . They (troubles) arise out of ourselves and the alcoholic is an extreme example of self-will run riot . . ." (AA, pg. 62).

The position of self-centeredness feels good for awhile and certainly feels even better using chemicals. This self-serving position within the family serves only to create inequality and power struggles between family members. As a result, love is erased because mutual fulfillment is impossible (Kushner, 1986).

Another important issue dealt with in the text of "Alcoholics Anonymous" and also in the meetings is accepting life without resentments. Resentments refer to feelings of anger, animosity, and resistance between people. With resentment there is a wall between people, and communication becomes impossible. The alcoholic's self-will position of wanting everything his way has to be met with resistance at times. This leads to a buildup of resentments, since the alcoholic/addict – especially an adolescent – cannot tolerate being told "no."

"It is plain that a life which includes deep resentment leads only to futility and unhappiness." (AA, pg. 66).

"I can't afford resentments against anyone, because they are the build-up of another drunk." (AA, pg. 325).

In the latter quotation, the message is clear that once a person again builds up resentments, that feeling of anger and animosity will move his or her mind away from the principles of the program and lead to relapse. Resentment places the "power source" in a youngster's life in the "wrong" place.

The Big Book also gives the spiritual answer for life difficulties: acceptance. Through acceptance, the alcoholic gives up trying to control the lives of other people and making himself miserable in the process. He also can allow people and situations to be as they are instead of taking a self-centered reference. In other words, looking at the world in terms of what exists rather than what one selfishly approves or disapproves.

"I need to concentrate not so much on what needs to be changed in the world as on what needs to be changed in me and my attitude." (AA, pg. 449).

Again, this reflects the realization that the problem is in oneself and in one's attitudes rather than in anyone else.

These principles are reinforced by other books published by AA, a magazine called *Grapevine*, and hundreds of books and pamphlets of meditation. One widely used meditation guide is called "Acceptance." It contains the famous Serenity Prayer:

God grant me the
Serenity to accept the things I cannot change,
Courage to change the things I can, and
Wisdom to know the difference.

*- Reinhold Niebuhr*

This prayer sums up the first steps of AA. It is one in which the focus is on the individual and his relation to God. The words "I" and "me" point to that. The message in the prayer is a very powerful one. It is asking for God's help to move away from selfishness and to be able to accept adversity without trying to control the situation and the person. Then the prayer moves on to courage and wisdom, in being able to decide what an individual can and cannot do. Acceptance, courage, and wisdom, though, can come only from God. In using this prayer, chemically dependent people are giving up the irrational belief that they have individual power. Power, the core issue for drug-dependent individuals, is placed where it belongs – with God.

The Twelve Steps of AA, the Big Book, the Serenity Prayer – all the elements of the AA recovery program are designed to lead a child to see that he or she is powerless over compulsions and over people and events. The AA program shows that the only real power any human being has is his ability to shape the way he feels about himself, the way he thinks. The personal power children are seeking comes from inside them. Those things that a child cannot control – and they include most people and events in the world – must be left to parents, adults, and ultimately to the Higher Power. Through AA, a child learns to care more about others than himself and to be flexible in his desires and demands on life. He learns to change these desires and demands rather than be broken by frustation and resentment. Ultimately, a child learns he is responsible for his own behavior and attitudes, his own happiness and unhappiness. Someone who understands that kind of personal power makes good decisions. Good decisions lead to confidence and self-esteem. That translates into healthy, strong adults.

This chapter is an interpretation of portions of Alcoholics Anonymous' Twelve Step program. The Twelve Steps to recovery are as follows:

1. We admitted we were powerless over alcohol – that our lives had become unmanageable.
2. Came to believe that a Power greater than ourselves could restore us to sanity.
3. Made a decision to turn our will and our lives over to the care of God *as we understood Him*.
4. Made a searching and fearless moral inventory of ourselves.
5. Admitted to God, to ourselves, and to another human being the exact nature of our wrongs.
6. Were entirely ready to have God remove all these defects of character.
7. Humbly asked Him to remove our shortcomings.
8. Made a list of all persons we had harmed, and became willing to make amends to them all.
9. Made direct amends to such people wherever possible, except when to do so would injure them or others.
10. Continued to take pesonal inventory and when we were wrong promptly admitted it.
11. Sought through prayer and meditation to improve our conscious contact with God *as we understood Him*, praying only for knowledge of His will for us and the power to carry that out.

12. Having had a spiritual awakening as the result of these steps, we tried to carry this message to alcoholics, and to practice these principles in all our affairs.

## Chapter Nine

Alcoholics Anonymous, Alcoholics Anonymous World Services, 3rd Edition, New York City, 1976, pgs. 59, 62, 66, 325, 449.

AA Membership Survey, Alcoholics Credit "Rehab" for AA Referrals, *Alcoholism and Addiction* Magazine, Quantum Publishing Company, Cleveland, Nov./Dec., 1987.

Bateson, G. "The Cybernetics of 'Self': A Theory of Alcoholism," from Steps to an Ecology of Mind, Chandler Publishing Company, New York, 1972.

Clinebell, H. Growth Counseling, Abington Press, Nashville, 1979.

Collins, Vincent. Acceptance, Abbey Press, St. Meinrad, Indiana, 1986.

Cocores, J.A. Co-Addiction: A Silent Epidemic, Psychiatry Letter, Fair Oaks Hospital, February 1987.

Gold, M.S., and Vereby, K. The Psychopharmacology of Cocaine, Psychiatric Annals, 14 (10), 1984.

Hamel, R.A. A Good First Step, Comp Care Publications, Minneapolis, 1985.

Jellineck, E.M. The Disease Concept of Alcoholism, Hillhouse Press, New York, 1960.

Johnson Institute, Family Enablers, Johnson Inst., Inc., Minneapolis, 1982.

Kerr, P. "Anti-Drug Programs Often Miss the Mark in Classrooms," *New York Times* News Service, reported in the Memphis *Commercial Appeal*, Sept. 19, 1986.

Kushner, H. When All You've Ever Wanted Isn't Enough, Pocket Books, New York, 1986.

Mann, P. "We're Teaching Our Kids to Use Drugs," *Reader's Digest*, New York, 1987.

Miller, N.S. A Primer of the Treatment Process for Alcoholism and Drug Addiction, Psychiatry Letter, Fair Oaks Hospital, July 1987.

Reiners, K. There's More to Life Than Pumpkins, Drugs, and Other False Gods, Woodland Publishing, Wayzata, Minnesota, 1980.

Steinberg, J. The Role of AA in Treatment and Recovery of Impaired Professionals, Maryland Medical Journal, Vol. 36, No. 3, March 1987.

Stuckey, R.E. Philosophy of Treatment, Fair Oaks Hospital, 1985.

*Rising from a test of fire, the spirit of one young person is shown to be strong and powerful at the conclusion of treatment.*

## CHAPTER TEN

# Treatment

RECOVERY FOR A DRUG- OR ALCOHOL-DEPENDENT TEENAGER IS A long-term, specialized family affair. Unfortunately, this country has been slow to respond with a coordinated approach to the unique problems teenagers present. As a result, few treatment facilities appear to understand the differences between a chemically dependent adult and a chemically dependent teenager. By the same token, parents should be warned that adolescent programs set up to treat emotional problems may not help their drug- or alcohol-dependent teenager.

Here's why adult programs do not help adolescents: First, adult alcoholics or drug addicts, once in treatment, generally seek out help. They realize their lives are out of control and they face certain destruction without competent assistance. Teenage alcoholics and addicts feel powerful and very much in control of the situation. They do not want to change their lives, no matter what they may say. Sixteen-year-old Tony is typical of the youngsters who come into treatment. At his first counseling session he screamed at his upper-middle-class parents: "I hate you! I hate you for putting me in this place." He began to get hoarse, and still he screeched: "I'll get out, you'll see. And I'll never give up drugs! Never!"

The resistant and rebellious attitude toward the need for change makes adolescents harder to treat than chemically dependent adults. However, there is a second major difference between an adult and a child, which a treatment program must be prepared to handle. The adult brain is more fully developed than a teenage cerebrum; therefore, an adult, no matter how deteriorated his condition, can be expected to have greater control over aggressive and sexual behavior during treatment.

These two main differences between adults and teenagers call for extremely divergent treatment methods. Unless a treatment program recognizes and has methods to deal with a teenager's peculiar characteristics, a youngster will not receive the help he or she needs to sustain a drug-free life.

Over and over again, I hear parents in pain make another mistake when they present their child for treatment: They have the wrong goal. They say they've brought their child into the mental health system to transform an unruly, disobedient, self-destructive teenager into a drug-free youngster who listens to them.

Psychiatric programs that are not Twelve Step-oriented treat emotional problems as the "underlying" problem and thereby may actually enable drug-using behavior. Likewise, treatment is not obedience school. Beware of those programs that claim easy solutions with behavior modification or learning therapy.

The proper goals and clear expectations that parents must have for treatment are: to get the youngster off drugs and alcohol, to create a new belief system inside him, and to demonstrate how to be strong in that new belief. Those are extremely difficult goals. However, with the proper therapy, an appropriate program component, and hard work, they are realistic goals. Parents in pain who expect less are doing their troubled youngster a great disservice.

## Treatment Programs: Inpatient

A chemical treatment facility that understands the particular needs of teenagers will feature these programmatic components for the youngsters: vigorous physical exercise, demanding academic work, both individual counseling and group therapy, and involvement in the Twelve Steps of Alcoholics Anonymous. If a program truly understands teenage addiction, the treatment will include family counseling, parent education sessions, group support meetings for parents and, most importantly, consciousness raising for mother. These parental components are necessary because, realistically, parents who often are codependents need help as much as their children.

The first step to recovery is to place the child in a drug-free environment. Parents in pain should not be deceived into thinking the problem can be controlled with outpatient counseling if the child has a negative attitude and is dominating his mother. Sometimes, parents delude themselves into believing their youngster has a small drug problem — perhaps just a weekly joint of marijuana or a few beers on the weekend — and therefore an abbreviated treatment program will suffice.

Having "a little drug problem" often is just the tip of the iceberg. There is no halfway treatment for a chemically dependent youngster. The first step must be to place the child in a drug-free setting. Parents in pain with older teens may need a court order to force their youngster into residential treatment. This can be accomplished, but not without considerable emotional stress on the parents.

One type of treatment program for adolescent alcoholics and drug addicts is called the multidisciplinary approach or, sometimes, the medical model, which is combined with Twelve Step work.

In this approach, a psychiatrist, psychologist, counselor, educator, and an activities director meet to assess each patient and draw up an individual plan to treat each need. For example, the team might examine the child's chemical dependency and decide the goals for this portion of the youngster's problem will be both abstinence from drugs and an understanding of the impact drugs have had on his life. Aggressive, violent, or runaway behavior might be another problem that the team decides to manage through a program of physical activity, while group counseling builds the child's ability to cope with life's frustrations. A third problem assessed by the team might be the power structure inside the family unit; the goal would be family counseling that enables father to treat his wife as an equal partner in their marriage and helps mother to accept her new power.

The multidisciplinary approach must use the principles of Alcoholics Anonymous in its treatment and recovery. Specifically, the program needs a balance between the mental health staff and recovering addicts who have years of recovery behind them. These recovering addicts and alcoholics model sober, straight behavior and are the chief instructors in spirituality as conceived by AA. These role models need to be on staff and available to the youngsters on a continual basis.

Spirituality is introduced in the comprehensive treatment of both the chemical dependency and the emotional problems of the youngster. Such a spiritual component is necessary, since the treatment professionals will be uprooting the child's destructive belief system, and the youngster therefore will need something equally as powerful and attractive to put in its place.

In addition to the multidisciplinary approach, parents in pain have available the Minnesota model of treatment, one of the earliest approaches to teenage addiction. Carried out skillfully, this treatment model also can be helpful for chemically dependent youngsters.

At the heart of the Minnesota model is a core of recovering alcohol and drug counselors, authority figures who show youngsters that life after drugs is possible and desirable. The actual therapists are recovering addicts and alcoholics. The doctor in the treatment facility may be one who cares for the patients' physical health and not a trained child psychiatrist.

The child's addiction is treated – quite properly – as a life-long disease, and the treatment professionals use the 12 Alcoholics Anonymous recovery steps as the method of controlling this disease. Often, youngsters are required to work on the first several steps of AA before they go on to the remainder of the program.

Clever youngsters can pick up the jargon and feed the counselors the required response. This translates to feelings of success in the child, unless the treatment professionals can discern whether the child is sincere or merely trying to fool them. If the program is an especially good one, the youngster will understand that he has a disease that he has to fight all his life and that aspects of the AA program apply to him. The key here is that the youngster must make a fundamental change in his mental attitude toward authority and power.

The Minnesota model can work successfully for youngsters if three criteria are met: parents are counseled; the program is tightly controlled to ensure no drugs reach the child from the outside world; and a solid aftercare support system is established for both parents and children. It is important that the program has been in existence for a period of time and has a good reputation.

The two best treatment models today show more similarities than differences. The quality multidisciplinary programs increasingly are employing recovery staff, and Minnesota model programs are employing more psychiatrists and psychologists.

## Therapy Methods: Outpatient

Just as there are choices in programs, so there are choices in the kind of therapy children can receive. Since each approach has its drawbacks as well as its strengths, most successful adolescent programs employ a combination of therapies.

One word of caution: Parents in pain should be warned away from any type of counseling or therapy that sides with the child and makes the parent feel somehow responsible for the child's chemical abuse. Such therapy will not make parents feel strong or confident in dealing with their teenager. Besides, it is a perpetuation of the great lie that parents must bear the blame (or glory) for the way their children turn out.

The other type of therapy to be avoided is individual counseling that expects the adolescent to respond by forming a "trust" relationship with the therapist. If the adolescent and his therapist appear to be getting along too well in the initial weeks of therapy, the professional has failed. Stripping away the teenager's belief system is part of the goal of therapy. Such a fundamental and painful change cannot be accomplished through agreement and conciliatory behavior on the part of the authority figure – in this case, the therapist.

What, then, are the most successful methods of adolescent therapy?

The cornerstone of any adolescent therapy was stated earlier in the negative. Here it is in the positive: Successful counseling is dependent on the strength of the counselor and his or her ability to establish a no-nonsense, show-me attitude with the youngster. The competent counselor may speak extensively with the parents and get a complete history before even saying hello to the youngster. Or, the counselor may see the entire family together before dealing with the youngster individually.

The successful adolescent therapist should be expected to keep parents up to date on the child's sessions. Any counselor who uses laws on confidentiality as the reason for not sharing information should be avoided. This may fly in the face of what many parents believe about confidential counseling. However, without complete honesty from the counselor, parents in pain could face the same situation as Zach and Abby. Their son Dan was 13 the first time he was admitted to a psychiatric unit for drug abuse and belligerent behavior. His doctor and counselor advised him to stay off marijuana and pills and stick to beer. Dan continued therapy on an outpatient basis and admitted to the professionals he was still smoking and drinking – but his parents didn't know. They didn't find out until he got in trouble for dealing drugs at school.

In addition to strong counseling sessions, successful adolescent therapy should include peer group counseling. This can be a very powerful therapeutic model for teenagers because youngsters are extremely aggressive in confronting each other's behavior. Unfortunately, it often is superficial and occasionally offers youngsters a way to avoid their own problems. They tend to deal with the trouble of others and ignore what brought disaster to their own doors. Youngsters in a peer group counseling session often have to be pushed by a competent therapist to deal with themselves in front of youngsters their own age. Many successful treatment programs and self-help groups such as AA, Tough Love, Al-Anon and others use this therapy in one form or another.

Individual counseling and peer group sessions are complemented and strengthened by multifamily therapy and support groups. These multifamily sessions not only are invaluable as treatment tools but also are a vital part of aftercare. In these meetings, the youngsters in treatment and their parents are confronted with problems by the therapist. The families help one another, and the sessions break down the feelings of isolation that parents invariably feel.

It should be noted that much of the success of therapy depends on the professional who works with the child. Today, most mental health care professionals are trained in a traditional, passive approach to counseling. Such an approach will not be effective with unreasonable, self-willed teenagers. The passive therapist will neither change the youngster's belief system nor alter the power structure in a family. When a child comes in for drug or alcohol abuse treatment, the adolescent is feeling strong, while his weary mother is usually struggling alone. She needs an ally, not another critic or impartial observer. Fundamental changes in an addictive child's universe must be made before a teenager can cope and survive in a drug-free world. Such a conversion cannot be accomplished by a therapist whose only contribution is: "And how do you feel about what Johnny said, Mrs. Smith?"

## Guidelines to Quality Programs

A truly effective program is balanced. Recovery staff and mental health staff must work together, for each has a unique contribution. Recovering staff members are the role models for the program. They live the program for the young patient and therefore are most effective in motivating them to continue in AA after treatment. Recovering staff must have several years of sobriety, regularly attend their own meetings, and have some interpersonal stability in their own lives. There needs to be both male and female recovering staff, who believe that the principles of the program will help young people. They must not become professional enablers by siding with the young person against the parent. Even if one parent is an active alcoholic or even abusive, siding with the youngster against the parent will only lead to trouble. Recovery staff can interpret and explain Big Book principles and slogans and help with Step work. A program without recovering staff is not a recovery program, even if the young people are given the materials and go to meetings.

The mental health professionals are in the best position to help the young person experience feelings, tolerate frustration, and learn to deal with the pain of giving up being Numero Uno. The mental health person also can deal effectively with the family on a personal level rather than merely educating the family about the family illness. In addition, the mental health staff members show chemically dependent young people that they can be accepted as people. Many youngsters are so filled with feelings of guilt, poor esteem, and low self-worth that they feel they never will be accepted by "earth" people. Most important, there needs to be a psychiatrist – preferably a child psychiatrist – who is well trained in development and family systems, who accepts the disease concept of alcoholism, and who can work with recovering staff and recovering professionals. Few programs have such a person, but the ones that do are usually outstanding. These professionals become well-known to the disciplines of psychology and psychiatry as well as to the recovering professional community.

Select a treatment program, then, with a well-trained and qualified staff. In order to assess their qualifications, inquire about licenses, degrees, and professional society membership. A professional will choose membership in those organizations that most clearly fit their own philosophy. In evaluating counselors, look for certification as alcoholism counselors (CAC) or substance abuse counselors (CSAC). Most of these counselors have solid training in chemical dependency and will belong to such professional organizations as the National Association of Alcoholism and Drug Abuse Counselors (NAADAC).

Evaluate the doctor. The program should have a psychiatrist who is trained and experienced in chemical dependency. Most bad experiences related by parents at Tough Love and Al-Anon meetings have been with psychiatrists or psychologists untrained and inexperienced in the treatment of drug problems. Whenever drug use is spoken of as a "symptom," and the underlying disorder is something else – beware! What that doctor is saying is that he or she does not believe in chemical dependency as a primary illness. While being treated for this "underlying" problem, the young person will continue to use. This is professional enabling at its worst and has affected so many people that even newspaper columnists have taken a position against such psychiatrists. The problem, though, is not in the profession of psychiatry or psychology, but in the lack of training in chemical dependency. Remember, it was Dr. Carl Jung, a famous psychoanalyst, who told a patient that traditional forms of treatment would not help alcoholism and that he must seek a spiritual experience.

Next, evaluate program philosophies. For example, effective programs recognize how physical troubled adolescents are and how this is reflected in everything from forming relationships to personal appearance. Sexual relationships are a form of addiction for troubled youngsters. For adolescents, "doing it" has much to do with acceptance and feeling good for the moment and little to do with meaningful relationships. Groups in treatment can be co-ed, but pairing off must be disallowed. Any sexual acting out should have serious consequences, and by no means should boys' and girls' rooms be too close to one another unless there is a staff member out in the hall at all times. The sexual tension in adolescent treatment is extremely high. Being aware of that and backing it up with strongly enforced rules shows the program is not afraid to deal directly with the patients. Likewise, overly aggressive behavior on the part of patients is not to be tolerated; otherwise the program will be laughed at by the teenagers. As one counselor put it, "There's no spirituality in your fists or between your legs."

When youngsters come into treatment, one of their major concerns is their physical appearance. If treatment is to be done economically – that is, in terms of time – there has to be a quick way for youngsters to feel positive about themselves. Looking good and feeling good physically is one such way.

Vigorous cardiovascular exercise once or twice a day will tone muscles and create a healthier body in the youngster. This improved physical condition raises the level of an adolescent's self-esteem. Unlike playing basketball or volleyball, cardiovascular exercise is something each child can do equally well, and success depends on individual effort – an important concept that teenagers need to grasp.

At the same time, a cardiovascular workout that sustains the heart rate up to three-fourths of its capacity for at least 20 minutes helps control the violent acting-out behavior that is such a problem in many adolescent programs. And it has one other positive: Strenuous exercise stimulates the brain's natural tranquilizers. As athletes know, endorphin neurotransmitters in the brain are released during hard workouts, resulting in a feeling of calm and contentment. Such a natural high is something troubled teenagers need to experience.

If the program understands adolescents and has staff to handle them, parents in pain should make certain the stated goals of the treatment are appropriate to the unusual problems of adolescents.

Parents in pain should insist on one goal: separating a child from whatever image he has adopted. For example, a boy who comes into treatment looking like bald-headed punk rocker Sid Vicious must be expected to give up the black leather jacket and let his hair grow out. In the same manner, a preppie who comes into treatment should have her curling iron and makeup taken away. A tough should bring all his heavy metal albums to the program only to have them confiscated by the program director. Knocking the props out from under the child's image is necessary to reaching the scared kid underneath the "cool" exterior – and there are several techniques for doing that. But parents should seek treatment programs that recognize the need to deal with the negative drug culture and provide rules about clothes, grooming, and entertainment.

Once the parent in pain discovers that the treatment program under consideration has a good staff, appropriate facilities, and goals in line with the needs of the adolescents, the next portion of the program to consider is the makeup of the family program. A good treatment program will have a smorgasbord of support groups, counseling sessions, and family therapy. A superior program will be able to demonstrate how these sessions can change the family structure.

Good counseling forces parents and children to confront their pain and frequently demonstrate – rather than discuss – how they feel, or the message they want to convey. For example, the mother and father of teenager Marty K. wanted to show their son that they had assumed control. Marty, a heavy metal rock music fanatic, projected a tough-guy image and lived up to his front by beating up younger children at school. To show Marty who now was the authority figure in his life, his parents elected not to talk about it again. Instead, they brought in all Marty's beloved heavy metal albums and tapes, put them in a plastic bag, and smashed them to bits while he watched. Next, they shredded his concert posters and his jeans with the fashionable hole in the knee. Afterwards, Marty was more willing to face his problems rather than hide behind the facade of a tough hood.

Counseling should not always involve the child. Parents in

pain have to remember they are also being treated for an addiction: their addiction to destructive habits and beliefs. Most common among these destructive belief systems is that women somehow are not as competent or as bright as men and therefore should be submissive to men. This almost universally accepted social belief pervades the drug culture.

In selecting a treatment program, parents should pay special attention to the way women in counseling and female staff members are treated by the program or institution. For example, an institution that employs staff members who work in women's rights organizations logically can be expected to deliver strong, positive support for mothers. Programs that do not deal with the need to strengthen mothers generally are a waste of time.

## Family Treatment

Every treatment facility has a different name for the counseling work that is done with families. Many insurance plans will not pay for counseling to help mother take charge of her offspring or to teach father how to back her up instead of overruling her. However, most insurance compaines will reimburse the cost of family therapy. Whatever its name, make certain the program under consideration features family counseling that is a cross between Al-Anon, Tough Love, and a mothers' consciousness-raising group.

Parents in pain should insist on parent education, multi-family counseling, or, at the very least, a parental support group. These groups air out feelings and break down walls of isolation.

Alice M. – whose daughter had been on drugs and alcohol, attempted suicide, slept with several men to get drugs, and pawned jewelry – kept a diary of her daughter's addiction. Of the parent support meetings, Alice wrote: "There were horror stories upon horror stories, and I came out of these weekly meeting sessions emotionally drained, but it was always a good tired. It hurt, but there was always healing with the pain." At one such meeting, Alice saw a mother confront her 15-year-old son with sexually molesting his 4-year-old sister and worshipping in a satanic church that sacrificed animals. Alice M. wrote, "I always left the sessions realizing how much I had to be thankful for and how much better my daughter's situation was than so many others."

However, it isn't enough that multifamily counseling or support groups provide parents in pain a sense of comfort and sharing. Some instruction must come out of these groups. These lessons should come verbally and through demonstration. The show-and-tell is most beneficial to the youngsters present, while the parents derive the most good from the verbal teaching of the professional in charge.

As an example of how multifamily counseling sessions work, consider one incident involving 14-year-old George, accepted by the other adolescents as one of the coolest teenagers in treatment. He sat in counseling holding his heavy metal music tapes and his tee shirts with demonic-looking musicians on the front. During the session, the therapist asked if he was ready to show the group he was becoming himself instead of just a tough guy. Suddenly George began to cry and hugged his tee shirts and tapes closer to his chest. Everyone in the session sighed with disappointment.

Then the therapist explained, "As long as they hold on to the 'cool' image, they won't recover. Feelings aren't considered 'cool,' and to recover you have to be able to deal with your feelings. If George goes back to school dressed like a hood, he's sending the message that these are the people he wants for his friends. It's easy to gravitate back to old ways – to using drugs – if you look in the mirror and see a druggie image. You don't hang out at Baskin-Robbins if you are trying to lose weight."

One of the questions that parents in pain invariably ask is, "How long is this going to take?" Inpatient treatment generally runs six to nine weeks with aftercare rehabilitation requiring two to three years. It simply takes that long to strip away a young person's belief system, plant a new philosophy, nurture it, and provide an insightful awareness of the physical effects of drug use. Any program that promises success in less time should be suspect.

Aftercare generally is the downfall of many treatment programs. Therefore, parents searching for treatment should be wary of a program that admits a child, treats him, then releases him without a strong plan for long-term aftercare. Such a plan entails coordinated support for the youngster at his school and in group meetings, both inside and outside the treatment facility. Aftercare means a commitment of at least three support and counseling meetings a week for parents and child.

Actually, good treatment aftercare programs never really end. Years after inpatient treatment, the youngster still should be attending such support group meetings as AA or Al-Anon – and Tough Love for their parents. Aftercare also should include a way for program graduates to readily contact a counselor or staff member at any hour.

Quality treatment designed for the special needs of adolescents is essential to recovery for a teenage alcoholic or addict. Such a treatment program should have highly trained staff, a variety of counseling models for youngsters and parents, support groups for teenagers and adults, strong academic and physical exercise components in a drug-free environment, appropriate goals for adolescent addicts to achieve, and an ongoing aftercare system.

Recovery takes time. And a lot of effort. However, if you as a parent are willing to make some adjustments and take charge of your own life, you will be strong enough to survive this ordeal – and your child will prosper from your example.

One 17-year-old recovering girl decribes her vision of chemical dependency as death, with the conclusion of treatment as a rebirth.

# CHAPTER ELEVEN

# The Spiritual Parent

IN DESPERATION ONE ICY DECEMBER NIGHT, MRS. M. WENT TO A support group for parents of drug-dependent teenagers. Mrs. M.'s 16-year-old daughter, Kathy, had become abusive and defiant, and was stealing and pawning jewelry. Still, Mrs. M. wasn't sure Kathy had a drug problem. She only knew she'd lost touch with her daughter, and that she was in pain.

"I had lost my ability to focus my thoughts on any subject for any length of time, or to follow through on any project," Mrs. M. wrote of that time. "I had lost all interest in life and was more dead than alive."

Like many parents in pain, Mrs. M. was spiritually defeated, a condition that rendered her powerless to assist her drug-dependent daughter. Yet, she saw parents at the meeting whose youngsters were in as bad a condition as Kathy, and these parents looked more sane than she.

At the parent meeting, a college professor told her, "We can help you to get control of your own life again. You can make it. We can guarantee you that. We can't guarantee that your child will make it, but if you can gain enough detachment and enough strength from this group, you can take control of your own life, and then maybe we can do something to help you save your kid."

Mrs. M. left the meeting with the Serenity Prayer from Alcoholics Anonymous and some hope. Gradually, she began to see there were some problems and conditions in the world over which she had no control. The guidance and outcome of those events was in the hands of a Supreme Being, a Higher Power.

And one of the things over which Mrs. M. had no power was

whether her daughter was a drug addict. That was something only her daughter controlled. Through her spiritual journey, Mrs. M. learned that one human cannot alter the internal workings of another human. To try was to become resentful and frustrated.

"Typically, I spent so much time trying to change things over which I had no control that my energy was spent and I didn't do the things I could have done. I had no discernment to know what I could and couldn't control," Mrs. M. wrote. "I had also become afraid of confronting Kathy, and I feared losing her love, which I needed as badly as an addict needs drugs."

As she began to gain support from the other parents, Mrs. M. saw that her attempts to help Kathy were counterproductive. Mrs. M. grew stronger in her belief that she could not change Kathy, that the Higher Power must act, and that her own life could be full without Kathy. As this belief grew, so did Kathy's respect.

"Mother, you're so cold. I've never heard you talk this way," Kathy said one night before she went into treatment. Later, she credited her mother's strength as the reason for her recovery. Her mother would say it was the Higher Power. Both answers are correct.

What every adolescent is seeking is a Higher Power. Some people call this spirit God, Buddha, Father, Allah, Jehovah, or simply It. The names are irrelevant, but the need for a positive spirituality is so strong that it is safe to say no child can grow up healthy and happy without the liberating joy that belief in a loving Higher Power brings.

And fewer youngsters still can recover from drug or alcohol dependency without this belief. As the French philosopher/writer Voltaire wrote, "If God did not exist, it would be necessary to invent Him."

Teenagers in trouble couldn't be more clear about their needs. Their adoration of heavy metal rock lyrics praising evil and their recognizing Satan as the master of their universe is as good as a flashing neon sign that says they find nothing powerful at the other end of the spectrum.

The difficulty with chemically dependent youngsters now is changing their minds – and the minds of their parents. When a youngster finds no joy in living, chances are the parents don't either. When a youngster believes himself worthless and friendless, odds are there is at least one parent who feels weak, isolated, and useless. Usually, this parent is Mother. Unhappy with other aspects of life, mothers wrap up their identity in children. Society views successful parents as those with successful children – and mothers have accepted this distortion. A mother who has a strong spirit and is satisfied with who she is apart from husband or child is happy, cheerful, and content that she is a powerful person. Such spiritually powerful mothers are like lionesses who are tough on the baby lions because the young are too unknowledgeable and immature to see there's a jungle out there. To those cubs, mother is God.

Spiritually defeated mothers give rise to troubled youngsters. The defeat may be in the form of an abusive spouse, or alcoholism, or poor self-image. The reason is immaterial; the result is the same for children. To prepare children for the journey of life, the spirit of mother must be strong enough to pass on to her children. Fathers who want their children to be competent adults must rally to mother's support. Society, which claims to want emotionally sound children, must stop giving these same children the impression their mothers are weak, second-rate humans.

A powerful, loving mother sets the stage for a belief in a powerful and loving God. She recognizes her control is limited and that authority actually rests with a power higher than hers. She is able to project this confidence to her children through detaching herself from problems she cannot change. Her attitude must be, "I have done my best – which is considerable – and now it is up to God."

The Higher Power, although ever-present, is quite elusive to most adolescents. So many substitutes abound. Formal education emphasizes that getting a diploma means a good job and good money. Radio, television, and their commercials emphasize nonvalues, instant gratification, and beauty through use of various products. Sex education is such a controversial issue that children learn about physical love in the streets. Most religions project no joy, are too strongly identified with the adult world, and sometimes promote the idea that men should rule women.

Youngsters find religion either unappealing or filled with charismatic demagogues who suck in dollars like high-power vacuum cleaners. Psychology with an emphasis on behavior teaches control over other humans, while psychiatry invents more potent drugs to control what psychology can't.

A strong spirit comes from none of these short-term gratifications. Instead, spirituality manifests itself in detachment from things that one cannot control and lies in acts of concern for others. Part of caring for others means keeping in good physical and spiritual health personally – the idea being that a "sick" person makes a poor nurse. When someone becomes a weight, it is an instinctive act of self-preservation to get away and restore personal balance. This is never more true than in the case of parents with a chemically dependent adolescent. Mothers and fathers who want to care for their children must first "care" for themselves and one another as worthwhile humans.

Caring for someone often leads to hard decisions for parents. Mrs. M. finally got her daughter into treatment. She told Kathy she was old enough to sign herself into treatment, or Mrs. M. could have the juvenile court commit her. But in any event, Kathy couldn't come back to her home until she was drug-free. At first, she was terrified her daughter would choose the streets – and in fact Kathy did rent an apartment and pack her bags. Still, Mrs. M. held fast to her spirit. Mrs. M. said later, "I got down to the roots of my anxiety, the fear that gripped me and caused me to do rescue operations and run interference to prevent Kathy from getting hurt or hurting herself. I discovered that I was afraid of the pain myself. I didn't want her to hurt and me to hurt too."

Parents have to accept a lot of pain to get their children out of trouble, but this demonstrates a powerful spirit. In the long run, the parent who refuses to be abused by a manipulative teenager is showing her youngster strength of character and demonstrating concern for the child on the highest level. It is easier – far easier – to assist an out-of-control youngster than to go through the anguish of straightening him out.

A parent who puts a child in treatment for chemical abuse but takes no steps to change her own self-image is like a woman who mops the floor but continues to let the sink overflow. As the college professor told Mrs. M. at her first parent support meeting, spiritual recovery for parents is a necessary prerequisite for the child getting well. A recovered mother becomes the lioness who wields the power necessary to keep the cubs out of the dangerous jungle. Helping a child help himself then becomes the highest form of love and demonstrates the strength of the spirit far better than anything else.

Getting hold of the spirit, what might logically be called the instinctive intelligence inside each human being, means looking for it. In self-help groups, particularly Alcoholics Anonymous, the Higher Power is seen as God-as-Each-Person-Understands-Him. That is very much a personal relationship unfettered by theological teachings or dogmatic practices. For youngsters, the search for the Higher Power begins with mother. They not only take their cues on the nature of God from mother, but to them she is God on earth. This is true most obviously for very young children, but the concept continues through adolescence. Only if mother is the dominant force and protector in their lives can the concept of God make sense to children and adolescents. Since children look to mother for protection and guidance, if she fails them it necessarily follows that God fails them.

At first glance, this might seem an awesome burden for any woman to bear. However, spiritually strong women have their authority vested in a Higher Power. This belief in a loving Higher Power allows spiritually strong mothers to move freely in a dangerous world, helping those they can help, protecting their children from negative influences, defying convention if necessary, and leaving the consequences to the Higher Power. Thus, mother models the spirit for her children and projects onto them the idea of a loving, caring Higher Power.

Organized affirmation of this Higher Power at work can be found in any group that allows free interpretation of the spirit and does not limit it by acts that humans can do. For example, a loving Higher Power comes to each one in the form that individual can accept; it does not restrict itself to those who read a certain book, pray a particular kind of prayer, or worship in a special place. However, the spirit is renewed and refreshed in a group setting, and spiritually strong parents should make sure their troubled youngsters have such groups available. Typically, parents turn to Al-Anon, Tough Love, or AA.

The Higher Power that spiritual groups make available to troubled youngsters provides adolescents with a different authority for their behavior. This is most evident in the ability of these teenagers to control the limbic system. For example, youngsters know instinctively when something is dangerous, but they must make a rational decision not to try and find out why it is dangerous. It isn't consciousness at work – that's the rational mind talking. This still, small voice is instinctive intelligence, and it is Higher Power at work. This rational decision not to test the danger is strengthened and categorized by values and morals.

Most modern children don't need to be taught more values and morals; they need to make the values and morals they have stick. That is the responsibility of the child and the instinctive intelligence or Higher Power inside.

How children find spiritual strength is related in large measure to the bond they have with their mother and the fight she puts up against the negative forces in their lives. A mother sets up positive standards and uplifting values, affirms the child's worth as a person, and rejects the negatives that spew into the house through television, music, or peer groups. She does this by refusing to be swayed by negative influences in her own life and by setting standards for the behavior of her children.

Parents, schools, churches, temples, scout troops, and youth groups pour love, advice, values, and morals into a child the way a computer programmer fills a machine with reams of information. When the computer or the child is called upon to act on the information given it, the programmer or parent has to trust that the mechanics are working correctly. The difference between the child and the computer is this: The computer doesn't have to believe in itself to work, and the child does. Adolescents who continue to see mother as a Higher Power are properly programmed. When the moment comes, and they are invited to try drugs, have sex, or steal, the answer comes out, "This does not compute." Or the answer might just as easily come out, "I can't. My mother would kill me."

Children who believe they have a loving Higher Power working inside have a self-confidence that sustains them through even the most shocking circumstances. During the civil rights movement of the 1960s, a poverty-stricken black girl was among those desegregating a previously all-white Southern elementary school. Every day she was subjected to jeers, spitting, obscenities, and abuse from children, white parents, and some of her new teachers. Yet, when researchers came to talk to her, they discovered she felt no hostility, no animosity, and no loss of self-worth. She felt only pity for her persecutors, and she and her family prayed for them every night.

The little girl's story shows something significant about the Higher Power and the accompanying spirituality that children need to grow up balanced and strong. That black child was focusing on someone other than herself. She was praying for those who hurt her. She was thinking about helping those whites who spit in her face when she went to school. She cared about someone besides herself. She felt this way because her mother told her it was right.

Having strong spirit such as that of the little black girl comes from detaching those uncontrollable elements of life from one's repertoire of worries, focusing on the needs of others, and keeping oneself above the negative influences of life.

Being a spiritually strong parent also means building self-esteem and confidence in a child so that those things that could tear down a child's self-worth are minimized. Some of the dangers to a child's self-worth have already been listed as destructive rock music lyrics, peer pressure, some programs or ads on television, and, most of all, drugs.

Some of the danger to an adolescent's self-worth begins when he is very young. So often, there is a negative and resentful attitude in children that is a subtle sign of bad things to come. In a sense, it is almost a self-fulfilling prophecy. These youngsters act as if they are not happy and that they never can be, so the prophecy is fulfilled. They seem to be angry, sullen, negative, and resentful. They appear defeated. Their spirits are weak.

These are the children to whom mother must assert her positive influence by developing self-esteem. She must point out to the resentful children that, ultimately, they are responsible for their own happiness. She can show them the times they have succeeded at some endeavor and focus on the good in them rather than the failures or shortcomings. Children, like adults, should not concentrate on the negative in life but rather on the positive. That too is part of the strong spirit.

Another aspect of spiritual parenting is letting children gain confidence through experiencing the consequences of their actions. Most parents would give anything to save their children from the embarrassing moments, the tearful feelings of being left out of the group. Mothers and fathers forget that their children are not reliving their parents' lives but an entirely new existence. It is a right of passage in that existence to earn self-confidence through mistakes and embarrassment.

Mrs. M. remembers getting to the roots of her anxiety, her fear about Kathy, in one of her first parent support group meetings. By working with other wounded parents, Mrs. M. finally decided that she had mounted rescue operations for Kathy throughout her life to avoid feeling the pain of watching her daughter suffer.

"I didn't want her to hurt and me to hurt too. I learned that real love is not suffering "for" someone but "with" the person. Real love is suffering with the person and knowing there's nothing you can do to stop or prevent the pain," Mrs. M. wrote.

What Mrs. M. learned in her support group was to focus on the needs of other parents in pain and gain strength through their common suffering, to allow her daughter to earn her right of passage by suffering consequences, to feel the pain of her daughter's hurts, and to let the Higher Power control those things out of her own reach.

"Changing feelings of panic to serenity is a great challenge to us all as parents," said Mrs. M. "To quit overprotecting and manipulating and release our children with love is the business we're about . . ."